JESUS

LOVES

YOU

LOVE

HIM

BACK

MICHAEL HIGGINS

Jesus Loves You
Love Him Back

Published by Michael Higgins

COPYRIGHT © 2018 Michael Higgins
www.lovehimbackbook.com

All scripture quotations are taken from the Holy Bible, New International Version (NIV) © 1973, 1978, 1984 by International Bible Society.

Library of Congress
Cataloging in Publication Data
Paperback ISBN 978-0-578-21085-8
Manufactured in the United States of America.

CONTENTS

3

PREFACE

My name is Michael Higgins. I was born and raised in Philadelphia, Pennsylvania. I do not have a college education, which means there are no fancy letters or titles before or after my name. Truth is, I barely graduated from high school. And I certainly do not consider myself to be a writer; not by a long shot.

But I do have a powerful testimony to share of how Jesus Christ rescued me out of a life full of drug addiction, pornography, and from a multitude of other sins. The man I am today can only be attributed to what my Lord and Savior did for me on the cross 2,000 years ago and is transforming me into today, by the power of the Holy Spirit.

You will see the word "miracle" used several times throughout this book. After seeing how God had completely delivered me from so many vices, in my opinion, the word "miracle" is the appropriate word to use. But let me just say that the greatest miracle to ever take place in my life—as is true with all Christ followers—is the miracle of God's salvation. That was when I crossed over from spiritual death to life and my soul was saved from utter destruction.

Had I been cured of drug abuse, smoking, pornography, and all other vices I was trapped in, and even if I fed the homeless every day of my life, if I died still in my sins, the end result for me is that I would end up in hell.

So, yes, God saving my soul from that wretched place was, by far, the greatest miracle to ever occur in my life.

Please be mindful of this as you read on…

I hope you enjoy…

PART ONE:

MY

LIFE

BEFORE

COCAINE

GROWING UP IN PHILADELPHIA

Are you ready? Let's go. As already stated, my name is Michael Higgins, and I am in love with my Lord and Savior, Jesus Christ. How could I not after He broke the chains of an out-of-control 20-year cocaine addiction?

As you will soon see, of all the addictions I've battled throughout my life, without a doubt, cocaine was the most destructive and overpowering of them all.

For many years, secular counselors tried convincing me that I wasn't a drug addict, that I was simply a victim of drug abuse.

I was told I had a disease, that it was the drug's fault more than it was my own. That worldly advice took me down a very dark and dangerous path that only God could deliver me from. And He did!

For the first 20 years of my life, I was cocaine-free. I knew what it was but, for whatever reason, I had no interest in trying it.

Everything changed when I moved to California. All it took was one snort of the white powdery substance and I was immediately hooked. Cocaine very quickly became my kryptonite.

But more on that later…

First, let me take you on a brief walk down my Memory Lane. The reason for this is that I want you to see that you don't have to be raised in a dysfunctional family to battle the same addictions I have in life.

As you will see, my family was far from perfect. Like all other families, we had our share of ups and downs and good times and bad times along the way. There were times when I felt I belonged to the best family on the planet. At other times, I feared the family might not stay together.

But in the grand scheme of things, from childhood all the way through to my teenage years, I was always well fed, clothed and loved.

I grew up in Philadelphia, Pennsylvania. I come from a rather large family. There were eight of us—my parents, four brothers and a sister. I spent most of my adolescent and teenage years

7

living in a small three-bedroom row home in the northeastern part of the city.

If you don't know, a row home is basically a cluster of small homes that are connected like one big slab, then sectioned equally. They all look the same. In many cases, the only difference between them are the house address numbers.

Having eight people living under that small roof wasn't always easy. Naturally, Mom and Dad shared the master bedroom. My sister—being the only female sibling—had her own room, leaving the five boys to share a bedroom. We had two sets of bunkbeds in that tiny room, forcing one of us to sleep on the floor. Having a little privacy, at least for us boys, was nearly impossible.

It wasn't exactly easy street. In fact, times were often difficult. But there was always plenty of love in the house and always enough food to eat. I am grateful to God for blessing me with two loving parents who always did their best to provide for us to the best of their ability.

Of all my siblings the one I was closest to, was my twin brother, Patrick. Growing up, we were practically inseparable. We did just about everything together. Nothing ever came between us. No matter how good or bad things were—we were always there to encourage and support each other.

To say that we were high-energy kids would be spot on. We always kept ourselves busy doing something, whether work or pleasure. Even before we were teenagers, we always had a job— whether it was paper routes, raking leaves, shoveling snow, painting fences, Christmas caroling, and everything in between.

In our free time, what we loved more than anything else was playing baseball. Whether times were good or bad, we always had the game of baseball to fall back on. We never grew tired of it. We even dreamed about being major league baseball players.

During summer months, hardly a day went by when we weren't outside playing hard ball, sponge-ball (as it was called), or wiffle ball for hours on end. If our friends weren't around (which was rare), we always had each other to play with.

We also played little league and high school ball, but the neighborhood games were the best. What I wouldn't give to be able to experience the innocence of those days again!

I truly believe if we had been encouraged more and stayed focused on baseball, something interesting might have happened.

I grew up in the Catholic church. Going to mass every Sunday wasn't something I did for spiritual fulfillment; I went because I was told to. For me, going to church was nothing more than a formality. We were told to "repeat after me," "stand," "sit," and "kneel." I knew what was going to happen before it happened.

My brother and I would usually leave during the Lord's Supper.

Because I didn't want to be there, my mind was always elsewhere. I never paid attention to the message—the formalities, yes, the message, no.

I remember the priest saying here is a message from the gospel of Mark or Matthew or Luke or John and so on, but my mind was usually a million miles away from there.

My brother and I were even altar boys for a while, but it didn't last.

Aside from the annual Christmas bazaar at church (one of the places I would go to purchase gifts for my family) or going to bingo with my mother on Monday nights (where I was promised pizza), the only other day of the year when I was excited to go to church was on Christmas Eve.

But again, in no way was this done out of spiritual conviction. If anything, it was more tradition than anything else, as it officially rang in the Christmas season. It was also the only time the entire family went to mass together as a whole unit.

After Christmas Eve mass, we would go home and have meatball sandwiches, cold cuts, salads, et cetera. Our friends would come over to eat with us. They couldn't believe all the gifts under our tree.

We would say, "This is nothing. The best gifts are under the tree downstairs." Christmas Eve and Christmas Eve mass were definitely a big part of our family's Christmas.

In addition to playing baseball, chasing girls, listening to rock n' roll music, drinking beer and smoking cigarettes, we were also pranksters. For the most part, however, they were rather harmless. And some were down right hilarious!

For instance, when I was 16, I worked at the local Red Lobster restaurant as an expediter in the kitchen. One evening, as I was leaving work, my friend and I decided to steal a live lobster from the restaurant and bring it to a keg party. The plan was to build a campfire and cook it there, but it never happened.

We got drunk instead.

Later that evening, at about 2:00 A.M., before calling it a night, I said to my brother, "What are we going to do with this lobster? We can't bring it home."

We finally decided against all human logic to place the still-alive lobster in a neighbor's mailbox. After removing the rubber bands off its claws, we lit a cigarette and put it in the lobster's mouth, banged on the Crawford's front door and hid behind a car across the street.

It didn't take long for the upstairs bedroom light to go on. Soon after that, a downstairs light was turned on. As we waited in anticipation, we couldn't stop laughing.

Finally, Mrs. Crawford opened the front door and turned on the outside light. Looking to her left, you can imagine her surprise seeing a lobster in her mailbox in the middle of the night, clawing at her with a lit cigarette in its mouth. If ever there was a moment where someone was caught completely by surprise, that was it!

We talked about that one for quite some time, not realizing we would be reminded of it 25 years later.

When my father died in 2006, my twin brother brought his kids to visit Mom Mom. While taking the kids out for a walk, he bumped into Mr. Crawford, whom he hadn't seen in more than two decades.

Mr. Crawford expressed his condolences, saying that our father was a very good man. He was right about that.

As they were saying their goodbyes, Mr. Crawford said to my brother, "By the way, we always knew it was you and your brother who put that lobster in our mailbox way back when. But it was so funny we decided not to tell your folks about it."

Even had they done that, my parents, too, would have laughed. Most of our pranks were of this sort of nature.

When three-way calling was born, it gave us a new way to mess with people. Believe me when I say, we took full advantage of it. Some of the victims we knew. Others we didn't know. Instead of being at the wrong place at the wrong time, they just happened to have the wrong phone numbers at the wrong time.

What we would do was call someone on the phone. As it rang, we would click over and call someone else, then connect the calls.

After saying their hellos, one would ask the other, "So, why'd you call?"

The other person would say, "I didn't call you, you called me."

Then the other person would say, "No I didn't, you called me."

This would usually go on for a while, until both sides eventually gave up and looked for other sources to blame. One woman tried reasoning that perhaps the phone lines had somehow been scrambled in outer space. Another woman blamed it on a new water filter unit she kept on her kitchen counter top.

But mostly, the callers blamed each other. Sometimes it would get heated. One person would tell the other person they were crazy or drunk or on drugs for thinking they'd called them.

We listened and laughed so hard at times that we had to cover the phones with our hands, so they wouldn't hear us. It was hilarious.

One day, we called someone we didn't know. When he answered, we said, "Eighth district police department (A local precinct in Philadelphia), how can I help you?"

The man said, "Excuse me? I didn't call you, you called me." He then politely said, "Maybe it's a bad line," and quietly hung up.

Two minutes later we called him back. Once again, he said the same thing and hung up.

After calling him several times, he became agitated and hit his boiling point. That's when we called the real 8th district precinct. Instead of saying hello, he started screaming and cursing at the woman on the other line, who happened to be a real police officer.

11

She said, "Sir, if you don't calm down and stop cursing at me I will send a car to arrest you."

"I don't care," he barked, "Stop calling my house. I've had enough of this!"

She said, "I have no idea what you're talking about!"

This made him even angrier. He eventually said, "Enough is enough!" and hung up on her.

We don't know if the police ever showed up at that man's house. Nor did we care to know. All we knew was that it was hilarious. Thankfully, they had no idea that we were behind the shenanigans, or that we were listening and rolling on the floor laughing.

My Uncle Jack was a frequent victim of our pranks. Aside from working for the city of Philadelphia, he also ran a gas station.

One evening, he was at home eating dinner with his family, when a man named Floyd—who worked with him at the gas station—called him. At least it appeared that way.

My uncle told Floyd he was having dinner with his family and left it at that. The next time Floyd called, my uncle asked him to stop calling him. Floyd replied saying that he didn't call him; the phone at the station rang, so he answered it.

After a few more calls, my uncle's patience came to an end. He accused Floyd of being drunk and warned him not to call again!

It was hilarious! What can I say? We were punks. Obviously, this was long before the advent of the Internet and cell phones.

All you young whipper-snappers out there reading this book probably have no idea what I mean. Even if you did, with today's technology, you could never get away with it.

Growing up with five brothers and friends with pretty much the same interests made life predictable. In addition to playing baseball and football, we would see who could get the cutest girl, who could drink the most beer, who had the loudest sound system, who had the fastest car, who was the strongest, and not necessarily in that order.

One particular evening, my next-door neighbor Tom had his high school graduation party at his house. We knew his parents were having a keg of beer, so we were definitely going.

As the party progressed, the drinking really got out of control. One of my neighbors, Dean, and I were quite drunk.

At the time, I was in 9ᵗʰ grade. Dean was in 8ᵗʰ grade. At about 2:30-3:00 A.M., on a school night we had words and ended up fist fighting in the street in front of my house.

My father, who was cured of alcoholism by this time, heard the commotion and rushed out of the house to break up the fight. We were swinging at each other wildly.

He pushed me toward the house and said, "You're drunk!" After ordering Dean to go home he told me we'll deal with this in the morning. He ended by saying, "I hope you throw up all night."

That's precisely what happened. Not only that, I couldn't sleep because the room was spinning, and I was scared to face my dad in a few hours. I had been drunk several times before that time, but that was, by far, the most inebriated I had been up to that point.

The next morning, while eating breakfast with my brothers, I heard my father's footsteps coming down the stairs. My heart was beating so fast I thought it might explode in my chest.

Even worse, when he came into the kitchen, my brothers went outside, leaving just my father and me. He sat down and calmly asked me, "Did the room spin last night?"

I said, "Yes."

He said, "Did you throw up?"

I said, "Yes, a lot."

He said, "How does your head feel right now?"

"Terrible." I said, "I'm sorry, Dad. I learned my lesson. It will never happen again."

My father said, "I'm going to let it slide because this is the first time. But if you go bragging to anyone that I let you off easily, you will be punished. Do I make myself clear?"

I nodded yes.

"You better get going," he said, "your brothers are in the car waiting for you."

13

As you might imagine, I had a rough day at school that day. Even worse, it was the beginning phase of my drinking for the sole purpose of getting drunk, for many years to come.

I've always had an addictive personality. My motto was, "I'll try anything once." Because of this, I experimented with many different drugs at an early age. But drinking beer and smoking marijuana were always my first two choices. Especially drinking. For the most part, my twin brother drank with me, though he never did drugs.

Back then, it all seemed innocent enough, especially since we weren't hurting anyone.

In high school, we were known as "the partiers." When people told us we were crazy, we took it as a compliment. The more popular we became in high school, the more sports started to take a back seat in our lives—organized sports, that is.

My brother and I weren't the best of students. We'd often cut class or skip school altogether. We even switched classes on occasion. Eventually, however, we stopped doing it because I wouldn't show up to Patrick's class, or vice versa. I honestly have no idea how we even graduated. Either the teachers really liked us, or they were just happy to see us leave.

Either way, we received diplomas. Go figure. At the time we started high school, there was great unrest and racial tension in the city. I remember eating lunch in the cafeteria with such a strong police presence, I often felt like I was in prison instead of in school.

That was during our freshman year. Over the next four years, the racial tension gradually eased. By the time we were seniors, it seemed everybody got along for the most part. The good news is that it gave us more people to hang out with.

We were well known by all and got along with everyone. We just wanted to have a good time. Because of our loose morals and ignorance to the Word of God, these times were truly awesome.

We were living in the world for the moment...and loving it.

SECULAR CONCERTS

It was during our high school years that we went to our first rock concert. The band we saw was Van Halen. It was the first of many concerts to come—the Rolling Stones, Journey, Ozzy Osbourne, AC/DC, Judas Priest and Iron Maiden, to name a few. Regardless of what concert we went to, we would totally get wasted on alcohol. At that time, I worked as a cook at a bar. In addition to cooking, I cleaned the bar and bathrooms on the weekends. Because of this, the owner gave a teenage punk like me keys to the bar. Big mistake!

Anyway, on the eve, or better yet, the early morning of a concert, we would go to the bar and grab anything we could get our hands on. This was usually around 4:00 a.m. when the bar was closed, and no one was there. We never took cases of beer for two reasons: One, because we had a long walk home; Two, if a police car drove by, they would easily spot us carrying the beer.

We took bottles of whiskey instead. This way, if a police car drove by, we could hide them in our jackets.

One day, we were going to see the Rolling Stones, Journey, and George Thorogood at the now torn-down JFK Stadium in South Philadelphia. It was an outdoor concert and more than 100,000 people were in attendance for it.

The weather was perfect; not a cloud in the sky. We got to the stadium early and started partying. I got so drunk that I passed out and had to be carried inside the stadium. George Thorogood was the first to perform. I don't remember his performance.

Journey was the next band to perform. It was then that I started coming out of my stupor. As soon as I could see straight, I noticed there was blood on my white T-shirt.

15

I asked my brother and friends what had happened to me. They said I kept trying to climb a small hill but kept falling and rolling back down. They said they wanted to help me, but they were having too much fun watching and laughing. The palms of my hands were bleeding from little pebbles that kept cutting into my hands each time I hit the ground, hence the bloody shirt.

At another concert, I was so drunk that I had to lean on my brother and another friend to prevent from falling down. My brother, seeing a Philadelphia police officer approaching us, told me to walk normal. It was like telling a fish to fly or a pig to swim.

I took one step and fell flat on my face, landing right in front of the police officer. My brother apologized and told the cop I had pneumonia. He didn't believe him, of course, but he let us go saying, "Get him out of my sight!"

At yet another concert—Ozzy Osbourne this time—we took the subway to the arena. We started drinking on the subway. One of our friends, being a real jerk, tried forcing a homeless man sitting near us to drink from one of the bottles of whiskey we brought with us.

We kept telling him to stop, that it wasn't cool, but he persisted.

One stop before the arena, the subway doors opened, and the police boarded the train. They quickly whisked us off the subway and confiscated our stolen whiskey. I thought we were going to be arrested—they even threatened to lock us up—but they eventually let us go.

But I didn't need rock concerts to feel the need to party. When my class went on a school trip to the Philadelphia Zoo, I foolishly brought a fifth of Southern Comfort along with me. Wanting to show off to my fellow classmates, I drank it in the back of the bus like it was KoolAid.

I was so drunk that I staggered into the zoo looking for a bench to sit on. After a serious bout of vomiting, a girl named Sherry sat next to me, where she remained for the rest of the day, rubbing my back and telling me time and again that I would be alright

16

(Personally, I'm not so sure I could sit there and watch someone throw up like that).

Sherry, if you ever read this, thanks again for your selfless acts of kindness to me that day.

SENIOR WEEK

Like I said earlier, it is truly amazing that my brother and I even graduated from high school. We certainly didn't deserve to.

Anyway. after graduating, we went to Wildwood, New Jersey for senior week. The sole purpose for senior week, at least to us, was to get wasted at the Jersey shore.

"Whatever happens, happens," was my motto.

After two days of serious drinking, while sitting on the beach, some of our friends had announced that they were going to do acid later that day. They asked me and my brother to join them. He answered no for the both of us.

When they left to do their thing, my brother was insistent that I not join them. I told him I understood, and that I agreed with him.

That evening, however, my buddies caught up with me. I don't recall where my brother was, but since he was nowhere to be found, I did acid with them. In addition to that, we smoked angel dust.

I was totally wasted! I'd never felt like that before. I felt like a giant who could fly!

We walked the boardwalk to see the lights and did some people-watching. We laughed hysterically at just about everything and everyone. There was this extremely obese woman wearing an all pink sweat suit walking straight toward us.

My one friend said, "Hey, look at the hippopotamus!"

We laughed even harder. When she passed by, we made a one-eighty and started following her, laughing the entire time.

She must have been totally humiliated. I would never do that in my right mind. Obviously, I wasn't a Christian back then. Now that I am, I feel shame whenever I think about that poor woman. If

17

I could meet her now, I'd get on my knees and beg for her forgiveness.

Later that night, we met two girls on the boardwalk, who invited us back to their hotel room. Four of us went with them, while the others decided to stay on the boardwalk.

These girls totally messed with our minds. They knew we were tripping. We drank beer with them and smoked weed. They turned all the lights out in the hotel room and squirted us with water pistols. Not only that, they used the flash from their camera to make it appear as if a lightning storm had materialized in the room.

Because we had lost complete control of our senses, we believed them. They had a music cassette they designed to totally mess with our heads!

For example: We were listening to Stairway to Heaven and were really into it. Suddenly, just as we started playing air guitar, the tape cut into a different song. We stopped, looked at each other, and laughed uncontrollably. When we regained our composure, we jammed to another song, and again it would cut into another song.

They even had velvet pictures hanging on the walls and black lights to make them glow. They were truly freaking us out in every way imaginable. It was as if they had bought a "How to mess with someone's mind on acid" kit and were making full use of it.

It was totally insane!

To this day, I never laughed so hard in my life. Even wasted, I felt safe in that hotel room. That is, until there was a knock on the door. We didn't want to answer it for obvious reasons.

Eventually, I opened it. It was my twin brother. Unbelievable! To this day I don't know how he found us—I never asked him.

Anyway, in an instant, I went from being joyful to paranoid. I pushed him out of the way, so I could escape his presence. Eventually I found myself hiding behind a dumpster at another hotel for several hours having the worse trip imaginable.

As sunrise broke, I sat on the beach alone. It felt like the ocean was breathing on me. That was the first and last time I ever took acid.

Of the 24-hours I was high on acid, only three or four were fun: the other 20 were terrible. Now that high school and senior week were over, it was time to start thinking about the future.

It was at that time that I went on a health kick. I stopped smoking cigarettes and drastically cut down on my drinking. I went to the gym every other day religiously. Working out very quickly became my new high. I was starting to look and feel better. Things were going good for me. I worked in several restaurants at that time. If I wasn't working, I was working out. No pain, no gain, right?

I've always had a talent for cooking. My late father was a chef. In this case, the apple didn't fall far from the tree, but I'll come back to that later.

One of the managers at the restaurant I worked at back then was a graduate from the C.I.A. (Culinary Institute of America). He thought I should visit the school because of my talent, he even offered to drive me there, so I could check it out for myself.

I gladly accepted his generous offer. My brother and another friend of ours joined us. I was very impressed and excited as we toured the campus.

On the way back home, we stopped in Manhattan. It was our first time visiting the *Big Apple* and we were excited. The man who drove us there purchased sniffing glue and encouraged us all to sniff it with him. What a rush it was! But for me it was a one and done deal. I never did it again.

When we got back to Philly, I felt certain that I would enroll at CIA. The problem was that I also had another dream: to become a rock star. Ultimately, that dream won out. Instead of going to school in Hyde Park, New York and training to become a chef, my brother and two friends and I packed our things and moved to California.

Our minds were made up. We were moving to Cali and there would be no looking back! I worked double shifts at the restaurant and even had two jobs, so I could save money for the move.

Up to that point in my life, I never had a serious relationship with a girl. I was having too much fun being single.

A few months before moving to California, my brother was dating a girl whose girlfriend wanted to meet me. I told him to tell her I was flattered but that I wanted to move to California a free man, with no strings attached.

Three days before we left for the West Coast, we had a going away party and this girl showed up. My brother introduced us, and we hit it off right away. She had an innocence about her that was refreshing. I spent my last three days in Philly with her.

We had a wonderful time together. Even so, I was still committed to going to Cali as a free man.

THE DRIVE TO CALIFORNIA

It's amazing how I can forget most of the things that have happened in my life, yet there are some things I can remember as if it happened yesterday. Moving to California is one of those moments...

On March 27th, 1985 my brother and I were about to leave the nest and drive 3,000 miles to our new lives. We had four drivers (my brother Patrick, Steve, Hal, and myself) and two cars to take us there.

My girlfriend came to my parents' house to see us off. At this early stage in our relationship, we were more friends than anything else. Even so, it was a very emotional goodbye. Many tears were shed that day.

Naturally, my mother was an emotional wreck. It was already difficult enough leaving our family for the first time. Seeing Mom so emotional made it even more difficult for us.

We left early in the evening. It was an unusually warm day in Philadelphia. Seventy-five degrees in the month of March in Philly is quite rare. Before driving off, my girlfriend gave me a handwritten letter that was 30 pages or so in length.

Since I was driving the first leg of the trip, I couldn't read it just yet. But even if I wasn't driving, my eyes were so full of tears, I wouldn't be able to read it even had I tried.

As soon as we got on I-95 southbound, the excitement kicked in. Our dreams were about to come true. Because of the unusually warm weather, we wore shorts and T-shirts.

We drove all night—taking turns driving, stopping only for gas, food, and to use the restroom. After 1,200 miles, we were exhausted, and we checked into a cheap hotel in Little Rock, Arkansas. We slept like babies that night and woke up feeling refreshed.

After eating breakfast at the hotel restaurant, we were back on the road. Fifty miles west from there, in the middle of nowhere, my car started overheating. We called a tow truck who towed us to a repair shop.

Five hundred dollars and three hours later we were back on the road. I know I got ripped off by this guy, but we were just happy to get back on the road. It was 80 degrees. Perfect! Driving on I-40 West, we started seeing storm clouds on the horizon. The farther we drove in the state of Arkansas, the more ominous they became.

All radio stations warned of tornadoes in each county we drove through. It was a sobering moment for us.

We never did see a tornado, but we encountered strong winds, heavy rain, and saw a few low-drifting clouds with a greenish tint to them. We battled the same inclement weather as we entered the state of Oklahoma. This slowed us down considerably. Even so, we decided to push on and drive through the storms to make up for lost time. The storms finally ended in western Oklahoma.

Between the car problems and the severe storms, we lost several hours of driving time. We eventually made it to the Texas panhandle. We stopped in Amarillo to eat and gas up.

When we got out of the cars it was 30 below zero with the wind chill. We were tired from a full day of driving so the cold air felt good on our faces. It really woke us up.

Seeing that we were wearing shorts and t-shirts, the locals looked at us like we were crazy. Before going to the restaurant, we changed into warmer clothes. After eating, we were back on the road.

The next state for us was New Mexico. When we arrived in the Land of Enchantment, the skies were clear but there was an inch of

21

ice on Interstate 40. At this point, we couldn't help but wonder what else could possibly happen?! I had a U-Haul trailer hooked up to my car that fish tailed several times.

As we inched along in traffic, we were determined to keep going no matter what. After many hours of cautious driving, we finally made it to western New Mexico to find the roads were clear.

It was time to make up time again!

One of the biggest landmarks we saw in the state of Arizona was a huge mountain range in Flagstaff, Arizona. It first came into view roughly 100 miles away. It took forever to fade from our view.

On April 1st, after driving through every weather pattern imaginable, we saw the "Welcome to California" sign. It was a monumental moment for us all. As we stood outside taking pictures, a bus full of girls drove by beeping at us, which only added to the excitement!

But that didn't change the fact that we were still six hours from L.A. and had no place to live once we arrived.

Thankfully, Hal had a brother who lived in Santa Monica, who let us stay with him the first two days. The one thing we had going for us is that we had jobs waiting for us in Van Nuys, located in the San Fernando Valley. Before we could start working we needed to find a place to live.

Since Santa Monica was 15 miles away from Van Nuys—with the suffocating traffic in Los Angeles, it might have well been 115 miles—we decided to go apartment hunting in the valley. After hearing so many no's, our luck was about to change.

We looked at a brand-new apartment complex in North Hollywood and told the owners we just moved there from Philadelphia three days ago. We had no credit; but we had jobs waiting for us in Van Nuys in the restaurant business. All we needed was a place to live.

In short: we needed someone to give us a break.

The two brothers who owned the building said they would take a chance on us. We signed a one-year lease on the hood of their car.

Talk about a relief! The apartment had two bedrooms and two bathrooms. Perfect. What else could we possibly ask for? We had a place to live in Southern California—yes!

We started working our new jobs a week later. This gave us time to unpack the things we brought with us and become a little more familiar with our new surroundings.

During this time, my girlfriend and I spent lots of time on the phone getting to know each other. We also wrote letters to each other.

Once we were settled in, she told me she was coming out to visit me. I was thrilled to hear that. Finally, we could get to know each other better in person. We did so much together in that short week—Disneyland, Knott's Berry Farm, San Diego, and several beaches, topping the list. We barely slept the entire time she was there.

It was during this time that we fell in love. On the day that she left, the drive to the airport was difficult for us both. She cried the whole time. I was sad as well.

When she got home, the letters and phone calls only increased, especially the phone calls. After a while, I got back into my daily routine. Life was good. It was about to get even better. Our father called one night informing that our family was coming to California to visit us the following month.

We were so excited! We wasted no time getting everything ready for their visit. When we met them at the airport, my brother and I could hardly contain ourselves. We couldn't wait to show them our new place. As it turned out, they weren't alone. Our good friends, the Alviras, flew to Los Angeles with my family.

I'll never forget it was a stifling 106 degrees that day. Anyway, they were pleased to see how nice and clean our place was and comforted seeing that our situation was stable.

Once again, we did so much in so little time.

When we dropped our family at the airport for the long flight back to Philadelphia, it was a sad time for us all. But knowing we would be seeing them again sooner than they thought, my brother and I weren't as sad as everyone else. And for good reason...

23

Every August, our family would vacation in Ormond Beach, Florida. It was situated just north of Daytona Beach. What they didn't know was that we would be joining them there. Only my girlfriend knew. And since my family invited her to accompany them, it was like having two vacations for the price of one.

When we arrived at the hotel in Florida my family freaked out, but in a good way. Our father was on the beach when he saw us and started crying. I'm writing this as if it happened yesterday and loving the innocent memories we created.

Those were some of the best days of my life. In the many years we spent at that particular hotel, our room was always party central. The bath tub was always filled with beer and ice, and we often partied until the sun came up.

But this trip was different for me. Mostly because my girlfriend and I were falling more and more in love. My family was getting to know her and love her as if she was already part of us. Love was my new high, to the extent that I rarely drank alcohol on that trip.

The worst part about the trip was that it flew by too quickly. Just like that, we were saying goodbye again. Parting ways with my girlfriend, not to mention my family, was extremely difficult for me. It was downright excruciating!

Upon returning to Southern California, my brother and I resettled back into the swing of things. Despite that we missed our family, life was good...

THE PHONE CALL

After six months of living in California, I received a phone call from my girlfriend. She was very upset. I asked her what the problem was. Once she was able to control her weeping, she told me she was pregnant.

Those were the very last words I wanted to hear come out of her mouth. She was only 19 and in nursing school, while I was 3,000 miles away and loving my new life.

Once she settled down, I told her I needed to make some calls and I would call her back.

The first call was to my parents. I told them I was driving back to Philadelphia and asked if I could stay with them until I got situated. I didn't tell them why I was coming home. I wanted to tell them in person.

They said yes.

Next, I called my work and filled them in. They understood. I called my girlfriend back and, with a heavy heart, told her I'd made all the necessary phone calls. After showering, I would leave for Philly. Talk about a surreal moment in my life!

I didn't want to leave the place I loved so much. But it was the responsible thing to do.

Two hours after our phone conversation, I was in my car for the 3,000-mile journey I'd recently made. Only this time, I was driving alone. It was around 10 p.m. PST. Needless to say, after being up all day I was already tired.

The first stop I made was at a 7-11 to gas up and get the biggest cup of coffee they had. As I was paying, I glanced at the cigarettes behind the clerk and asked, "What are the lightest smokes you carry?"

The man said, "Merit."

I said, "I'll take a pack of them."

The first time I smoked a cigarette I was nine. But like I said earlier, I stopped when I got on my health kick, approximately three years prior to this time.

After filling the tank with gas, I climbed inside the car and lit a cigarette. The first drag made me feel dizzy and high at the same time. As soon as I flicked it out the window I lit another one. Then another. And another. I was barely out of Los Angeles and I already needed more smokes.

Before you knew it, the sun was rising. I'd been driving a good eight hours by this time. I remember how it stung my eyes, but I kept driving. After a while, another sunrise took place.

I believe I drove 38 hours straight before finally stopping near Oklahoma City. I checked into a hotel and slept for about eight hours. To say I was a little loopy would be an understatement.

The next morning, after eating breakfast, I refueled and was back on I-40 headed East. My goal was to drive to Fairfax, Virginia and spend the night with friends before making the final leg of the trip.

By this time, I knew I was doing the right thing. I had this unbelievable peace in my heart. True peace and clarity.

Another thing different from the first time driving coast to coast was the music I listened to. Instead of rock and roll music blaring through my car speakers, I listened to Lionel Richie, because that's what me and my girlfriend listened to when we were together.

I was excited to see her and start our lives together as parents. There were no cell phones at the time, so I updated her periodically at phone booths along the way.

I made it to my destination in Virginia, thank God.

The next morning when I woke up, I only had 120 miles left to go. Compared to the nearly 3,000 now behind me, this was a hop skip and a jump. I called my girlfriend and my parents and told them I was headed out and would see them in a little while.

Upon arriving in Philadelphia, I went to my parents' house first to unpack and shower.

My father said, "You just did something I always wanted to do, drive coast to coast."

I said, "It was amazing!" My parents still didn't know about the pregnancy. I wanted to see my girlfriend first before telling my folks.

Driving to her house, I was quite nervous. Mostly because I hadn't met her parents yet. Since I met my girlfriend three days before moving to California, there was no time to meet beforehand.

When I arrived at the house, we hit it off immediately. They were a very likable couple. Her mother prepared a nice dinner and we enjoyed getting to know each other. Then came the bombshell...

The next day, my girlfriend told me she'd had an abortion while I was driving back from California. It was like a knife in the back. I was paralyzed and freaking out at the same time. I gave up everything for her in a matter of hours. Everything!

I have never experienced feelings and emotions like that before and I never want to again! I was devastated, truly devastated. I stormed out of her house and didn't talk to her for many weeks. She constantly called me, but I refused to talk to her.

My parents had no idea why I refused to answer her calls. They still didn't know about the pregnancy nor about the abortion. They assumed we were having an argument.

With my mind made up, I asked my father if he still wanted to drive coast-to-coast?

He said yes. He called his work and told them he needed time off to drive me back to California.

I finally called my girlfriend and told her I was moving back to California. This devastated her.

The last few weeks in Philly with her were great which made it difficult to leave her again, but my mind was made up. I was going.

BACK TO CALI I GO

Growing up in Philadelphia wasn't always easy, as I said earlier. In addition to struggling to make ends meet, our father was an alcoholic for much of his life. We saw our share of crazy things growing up.

My father wasn't a violent drunk, not physically anyway, he just couldn't stop drinking. I can still remember the constant arguing with my mother and the police coming to the house on occasion to take my father away until he sobered up.

I also remember when he showed up at our baseball game totally inebriated one day, forcing the coaches to ask him to leave. He even took us to the bar with him on occasion, where everyone knew him. His drinking even caused him to lose a few jobs.

Praise God, my father was delivered from alcoholism a few years before this time. He was clean and sober and was on top of his game. He even quit smoking cigarettes. Those who had mocked and scorned him for so many years now respected him. I'll even go so far to say that my father was an inspiration to so many.

Up until then, I never had a real relationship with him. So, as you might imagine this was something I really looked forward to.

Our conversation was totally awesome. The more we drove, the more we truly got to know one another. It was nice talking to my father the way I would a friend. I will always treasure that trip.

My father enjoyed it too. Like my first drive to the West Coast, we had our share of difficult adventures along the way, but we eventually made it to Los Angeles safely.

We went sightseeing then drove to San Diego to visit some of his friends. We had such a wonderful time together. Before I knew it, I was seeing him off at the airport.

As I watched his plane depart for the East Coast, I realized this was the closest we had ever been.

I remember feeling terribly alone. Part of me wanted to be on the airplane with him. My twin brother had gone back to Philly several months prior to this point. For the first time in my life, I had no family with me. Three thousand miles separated us.

It was just me and my roommate, and our relationship wasn't what it used to be. The apartment looked nothing like it did when I left a while back. It was dirty and empty.

I felt lonely and terribly alone and didn't know what to do with myself. And to think all this happened before I ever snorted a single line of cocaine. That was all about to change.

My life was about to enter a deep, dark abyss...

PART TWO:

MY

LIFE

DURING

COCAINE

HOOK, LINE, AND SINKER

After going through such a traumatic experience with my girlfriend, and with no family with me on the West Coast, the one thing I still have was my work. The company enthusiastically welcomed me back, and I worked as much as they would let me, including many double shifts, so I could start saving money.

Due to sheer boredom and loneliness—after all, there was no Facebook back then—I started drinking even more than I worked out. My attitude quickly became, "I don't care anymore!"

This is a dangerous mind-set for anyone to harbor. I didn't know it at the time, but because of this unhealthy way of thinking, my life was about to completely unravel...

One day in the middle of working a double shift, I was at the bar with one of my coworkers. No one else was with us. He put a huge line of cocaine on a plate and said, "Here, try this."

I knew what it was but said, "No, man, I'm good."

He reminded me that we had a long day ahead and this would help. I eventually caved in and snorted the white line. WOW! It was amazing. As already stated, I'd tried many different drugs up to this point, but nothing could compare to this. I didn't know it yet, but I was instantly hooked.

A week later, he offered me another line. I didn't hesitate this time. It gave me the very same sensation.

The following week, he offered it to me again and I accepted.

The fourth week I waited for him to give me a line to snort, but he never did. Eventually I asked him for it.

He said, "It's going to cost you this time."

I asked how much it would cost. He said $50. I handed over the money, took the bag, and went straight to the restroom and did a line. It didn't take long—only a couple of bathroom runs—but the $50 bag full of cocaine was gone.

I couldn't believe it. I bought another $50 bag, which means I spent $100 on cocaine in only one hour!

When work was finished, I needed more because I was going nightclubbing. I quickly understood why cocaine was called a "Rich Man's Aspirin."

This coworker was no longer just my friend, he was my main man. He had what I needed, and he knew it. The biggest problem for me was that I knew no one else in the cocaine business, and my dealer would only sell me cocaine at the restaurant.

So, even on my days off, I found myself driving to work hoping he would be there. There were no cell phones back then and I didn't have his home number. Nor did he ever offer it to me.

When he was out of cocaine, which happened on occasion, I was miserable. I soon realized I needed another connection.

One of the guys I'd partied with eventually introduced me to someone who sold me eight balls of cocaine. He quickly became my new best friend. Back then, an eight ball was an eighth of an ounce of cocaine which cost $275.00 a pop.

My first dealer had sold me some really good stuff, but this new cocaine was the bomb. Even better, he gave me his phone number and said he would even deliver to me. After placing an order on the phone, I paced back and forth in my apartment waiting for him to arrive. It always seemed to take forever.

The moment he rang the doorbell, relief washed over me. Before opening his briefcase, which held the drugs and scale, he wanted to be paid. With money in hand, he took the scale and measured the exact weight. No more, no less.

Between both dealers, I was pretty much guaranteed cocaine whenever I wanted it. Before I knew it, all my money was gone. My utilities were always being shut off and I was behind on the rent. My work was also suffering, and eviction was right around the corner.

My thinking back then was to find a way to make more money, so I wouldn't be evicted from my apartment, and I could still afford to support my cocaine dependency.

One day, instead of buying an eighth of an ounce, I purchased a quarter ounce of cocaine, then packaged four one-gram packages hoping to sell them to friends for $100 each, the going price at that time. Selling the four grams to my friends would allow me to get most of my money back, plus leave some left over for my own personal consumption.

Because of my new addiction, and due to my severely depleted finances, I could no longer afford to go out nightclubbing. But I was okay with it. I didn't need loud music or alcoholic drinks or women at this point in my life. All I needed was cocaine and cigarettes.

For someone who used to drink like a fish, this was rather remarkable. Suddenly, I could care less about alcohol. As long as I had cocaine in my body, all was well with the world...

Anyway, after calling two of my friends and telling them I had four grams of cocaine for sale, I did a few lines from my personal stash, hoping one of them would call to buy some or all of it.

I was wired for sound, and paranoid constantly looking out the window for the cops. By this time my personal stash was just about gone.

Finally, at around two in the morning, one of my friends stopped by with four one hundred-dollar bills to buy the four grams from me. Even though I still had the coke on me, I told him it was all gone.

The money I spent for the drugs was intended to keep my utilities turned on. All I had to do was take the money, give him the stuff, and say good night, but I didn't.

Instead, I told him he was too late, and that I'd already sold it. But in truth, I wanted it all for myself.

That's when I realized I was in serious trouble with no way of stopping the car from driving off the cliff, as the saying went. But instead of seeking treatment for my growing addiction, I kept on using.

In the following days, my utilities were turned off and eviction was right around the corner. I made more than enough money to pay my bills, but since cocaine had its full grip on me, paying bills was no longer a priority. Just like that, my life was spiraling out of control!

During this time, my girlfriend and I still spoke on the phone just about every day. Neither she nor anyone in my family knew how messed up I was! In just a few short months, I'd turned into a full-blown cocaine addict, which opened the door to many other self-destructive devices which soon took hold of me.

Pornography was at the top of the list. Whether I went to strip joints, peep shows, or I gawked at magazines and watched porno movies at home, it had a huge grip on me.

At this point, I stopped working out altogether. I drank at home if there was extra money. But if I had to choose between booze or cigarettes, cigarettes would always win. Go figure.

My relationship with my roommate was horrible at best. We went from being best friends to complete strangers.

One morning after waking up in a fog, I noticed a note on my front door as I was leaving for work. It was from my new neighbor. She accused me of hitting her car with mine and wanted me to pay for the damage. I went down to the parking garage to inspect both vehicles, all the while wondering what I had done the night before.

I was relieved to see there was no damage done to my car. Not even a scratch. I quickly concluded there was no way on earth my car had hit hers. There wasn't a single scratch on my car.

I asked my friend, Paul, to come to my place after work, to inspect both cars. He agreed and quickly surmised there was no way my car could have done that. He told me not to worry about it. He said she was only trying to blame me for something she had done.

Though certain I'd done nothing wrong, I had become extremely paranoid living in L.A. on my own. I had no car insurance, my tags were about to expire, my work ethics were going south, I was about to be evicted, about to have my utilities shutoff again, and I had no money to take care of my responsibilities.

Furthermore, I always feared the police would come knocking on my door at any moment and, if I didn't change my ways soon, I'd wind up either in jail or dead. It was time to get out of Dodge!

I told my girlfriend I wanted to move back to Philly, so we could finally start our lives together. She was so excited I was coming home but had no idea the man I'd become in just one short year.

33

I once again asked my father to drive coast to coast with me. I told him I was coming home for good this time. He was pleased because he really loved my girlfriend and wanted to see us together.

After calling work and getting the time off, he flew to LAX, and two days later we were driving back to Philly.

HEADED BACK TO PHILLY...AGAIN

Satan always seems to attack me most when I'm alone. Like I said earlier, the first six months spent in California were quite awesome. I had my twin brother with me. He was the best accountability partner I could ask for.

The last year on my own I had made a complete one-eighty. I started doing things I never would have considered had I been in my right mind. Suddenly those self-destructive things were consuming me from within and was starting to define who I was.

In short, I hated who I was becoming in the last year I lived in North Hollywood, California, and was in serious need of a fresh start.

My girlfriend was the answer. Like everyone else back home, she knew nothing about my cocaine addiction. With her help, even if she didn't know it, I would quit doing drugs, smoking cigarettes, drinking alcohol and watching pornography.

My father and I left for Philadelphia in February of 1987. I told my girlfriend I would try to be back in time for her birthday, which was less than a week away. Dad and I had another memorable drive together. Everything was always good when he was around. He had a way of making me feel safe and protected. He was such a responsible person at this stage of his life. I was so proud of him.

As for me, I had forgotten what being responsible was all about. Before leaving California, I requested a transfer to a restaurant back home. The name of the chain I worked for was Specialty Restaurants. Their restaurants were theme based, located all over America, and were quite successful at that time.

Thankfully, they were able to accommodate my wish. Instead of working in Northeast Philly—where I stayed with my parents until I got situated, I was transferred to a restaurant in downtown Philadelphia, on a ship called the *Moshulu,* at Penn's Landing on the Delaware River.

My father and I made it home from the West Coast just in time for my girlfriend's birthday party. This was the first time I'd seen her in more than a year. She looked great. Just one look and I felt I did the right thing by moving back home.

Before reporting for duty, I took a week off, so my girlfriend and I could catch up on things. We took full advantage of the time.

Aside from shopping for my new work uniforms, everything else was "us" time. I also got to meet many of her friends at her birthday party. Even though we had little in common, I liked them, and I believe they liked me too.

Life was starting to improve! I was cocaine free all week and this was the most clean and sober I'd been in roughly a year. Not only that, I was properly nourishing my body again and starting to feel good about myself.

MY NEW JOB

The general manager at the Moshulu Restaurant knew I was a good worker and could be an asset for her. I first met Pam when I worked for her in the Northeast Philadelphia restaurant.

Pam was a "no nonsense" manager. Without my knowledge, and to keep the other employees on their toes, she told everyone on the ship that I had transferred from one of the California restaurants, that I knew the owner, and that I would be reporting back to him.

In truth, it was all a lie. While I did work with the owner's son, I didn't personally know his father.

At any rate, my first day on the ship was a bit unusual. Normally, I fit right in, but this time everyone was acting strangely towards me. The next day someone asked if I was a spy for the company.

35

I told them I was not, and asked, "Why would you ask me that?"

He told me the things Pam had said to the employees and I just laughed and said, "LET THE GOOD TIMES ROLL!"

It was like music to his ears! Once again, I was the life of the party. It didn't take long to learn that the ship was a huge drug haven. After my shift was over, I would go to 2nd Street for drinks with my new friends. Second Street is comprised of several blocks of restaurants and bars located in Center City, Philadelphia.

This was the place to go for restaurant workers who wanted to unwind after serving customers all night. Some bars had after hours clubs on the second floor that were open until 6 am.

Since we didn't get out of work until 11:00-11:30 p.m., those clubs became part of our nightly routine. It was there that I was reintroduced to cocaine, forcing me once again to live a double life.

It was impossible to avoid the white powdery substance; many who worked on the ship snorted it.

My girlfriend and I had completely different schedules. She woke at 5:00 a.m. to start her day. Most nights, I wasn't even home at that time. When she returned from nursing school, I was just waking from a long night of partying. Not only that, while she was free on the weekends, that was my busiest time at work.

Sleeping in the basement of my parents' house allowed me to quietly sneak in the back door most mornings. It didn't take long, however, for my folks to suspect that something was going on. I think they just thought I was drinking too much.

Another thing my girlfriend didn't know was that I was constantly partying with the waitresses and cocktail waitresses at work. It oftentimes led to other things.

The guys on the ship were also fun to be with. We quickly developed a system for getting cocaine. At the end of our shift, as the rest of us did side work, one of us would leave the restaurant and drive to 18th and Wallace to purchase cocaine for everyone.

The side work we did was both tedious and time-consuming. On top of that, we were checked out with flashlights. If one glass or piece of silverware had marks or fingerprints on them, the managers made us start all over again.

After a long day at work, we were itching to party. When the delivery person made it back with the goods, we were all smiles, and thankful that he made it back safely without getting busted.

This went on for quite some time. I cannot speak for anyone else but when I ran out of cocaine, I always got more before going home.

Some of us even had a money-making scam going on at work, involving the chef and some of the cooks. We usually did it with larger parties. After handwriting the orders on paper, we would give it to the cooks involved without ever ringing it up on the computers.

They, in turn, prepared the food and quickly got rid of the evidence. When it came time to pay the bill, we told the customers the computers were down, so we had to handwrite the check.

They never questioned it. If they paid in cash, everyone involved got their cut. If they paid by credit card, we were forced to ring the order up. Even though God has forgiven me for this, each time I revisit this extremely sinful time in my life, I still feel shame.

Something else we did that I'm not proud of happened topside one night where the employees went to smoke cigarettes. After lighting up, we noticed a money pouch that hadn't yet been dropped into the safe. One of us opened it to find cash stuffed inside. With no managers around and with no cameras spying on us, we didn't think twice about taking the money.

As it turned out, there was roughly $300 inside the pouch, which we used for more drugs. In retrospect, even if it was three-million dollars, it was the wrong thing to do. Anyway, before leaving that night, the managers were frantic asking everyone where the money was. We denied knowing anything about it, but I'm sure they suspected it was someone from our crew.

The next day, as I was getting ready for work, I received a call from one of my buddies. He said, "Don't come to work. The police are here waiting for you and everyone else suspected in the theft."

I never stepped foot inside that place again. I had worked for this company for several years in four of their restaurants—two in Los Angeles and two in Philadelphia. Because of my sheer stupidity, all that hard work went down the drain. I was nothing to my employers now, and rightly so. While the turkeys I worked with were just as guilty as me, I had only myself to blame for my foolish actions.

Thankfully, I never heard from the police...

Suddenly out of a job, I had to think of a good lie to tell my parents and girlfriend. I can't remember what lie I told but it worked.

I soon realized having a pocketful of money and keys to a car was a dangerous combination for me. So, I decided to go back to working as a chef. The hope was that, by getting a paycheck each week, instead of cash each night, I would be a little more responsible.

As you will soon see, it didn't take long to discover that when addicted to cocaine, one will find any means necessary to obtain it.

But unlike in California, now that I was back with my family, I had to keep covering my tracks.

TIME TO GET MARRIED

I started working at Nick's Roast Beef House as a cook. Once again, I quickly became the life of the party.

As I said earlier, my girlfriend's work schedule was different than mine, so most of my partying went undetected by her. I had my own apartment at this time, so I didn't have to worry about sneaking in or out of the house anymore.

The problem was I wasn't paying my rent or other bills, so in a matter of months I was evicted from the apartment.

This was also the time I learned my girlfriend was pregnant. We decided that, with a baby coming, and knowing we would soon be married, I should move in with her. My parents were the first to know about the pregnancy. They knew we loved each other but I believe they had reservations about the marriage and about me being a father. I lived in their home long enough for them to know I had a problem. They just didn't know what it was.

Her parents, on the other hand, were still in the dark about the pregnancy and my growing addiction. When we informed them that we were expecting a child, they were excited.

It was time to get married. Knowing my girlfriend didn't want to show in her wedding dress—meaning she didn't want everyone to know she was pregnant—we had very little time to work with.

We went to marriage classes and planned on being married in the Catholic church she went to, but when they became aware of her pregnancy, they said they wouldn't do it.

That didn't sit well with me. The church claims that abortion is a sin, which it is, but we wanted to do the right thing and get married before the baby was born, yet they wouldn't marry us in her church. Thankfully, a priest we knew from another Catholic church welcomed us with open arms. As we planned for our wedding, which was set to take place in four months, I was promoted at work.

The owner of Nick's Roast Beef House asked me to be the head chef at his other restaurant. I gratefully accepted the offer and thanked him for believing in me. I worked long hours, especially in the beginning, rearranging the kitchen to my liking.

I excelled at creating the menu items and daily chef specials. If it weren't for my severe cocaine problem—which no one at work knew about—my life would have been perfect.

My future wife came in on occasion to join me for lunch or dinner. She loved being pregnant. She was radiant, and she never complained about anything. Now that we were living together, I had to account for my money, time, and actions.

I was always exhausted, but I worked hard despite it all. I was a good liar. I could pretty much cover anything up. I was believable.

I would call my soon-to-be wife at the end of my workday and tell her I would be leaving work in an hour or so and wanted to say good night and tell her I loved her because I knew she had to wake up early.

The moment the call ended, I was off to score cocaine to take home with me. Most times, she was already sleeping when I got home. I would give her a kiss, shower, then go downstairs to party all by myself. Pretty pathetic, huh?

That was my goal but most times it never happened that way.

During this time, my cocaine usage was under control. I truly thought because of my future marriage, a child on the way, and my new job which I truly loved would help me stop using. This mindset was an easy trap for me to fall into.

Time really flew by, and before you knew it, it was just about wedding time. My bachelor party was great. There were no strippers, no drinking, and no drugging. My brothers and I went to an Eagles football game, followed by dinner after the game.

The night before my wedding, my twin brother and I went out for a night of drinking. What he didn't know was that I was also coked up; certainly not a good way to enter into the holy and sacred bond of matrimony!

As you might imagine, I felt groggy the next morning, but it gradually wore off. We had a beautiful wedding ceremony followed by a festive celebration party. Even better, we were headed to Hawaii for a two-week honeymoon. Life was just perfect.

As a wedding gift, a good friend of mine paid for the limousine that transported us everywhere we went that day. His generous gift also provided limousine service to the airport two days later and back when our honeymoon was over.

It was a generous wedding gift to be sure.

Our honeymoon started in Honolulu on the island of Oahu. Having already been to Hawaii, I pretty much knew where to take my wife sightseeing.

Roughly five days into our honeymoon, I was getting antsy and wanted cocaine. One night, after my wife fell asleep, I walked Waikiki Beach asking people where I could buy cocaine. No one helped me. I'm sure many thought I was a cop.

After a while, I grew tired and went back to the hotel, to find my wife awake wondering where I went. I told her I couldn't sleep, and I took a walk on the beach. As always, she believed me. Lying in bed that night, I realized that night that I probably wouldn't be able to score cocaine in Hawaii. I accepted it and enjoyed the rest of our honeymoon.

The second week we went to Kaanapali Beach on the island of Maui. We had an awesome time, absolutely awesome!

The day we flew back to Philadelphia we arrived at the airport in Oahu, checked our bags, then went to get breakfast. After breakfast, we went to our gate to learn that the plane had already left without us. Worse, our luggage was already checked onto the plane.

The airline booked us on another flight back home. As it turned out, we landed in Philly two hours before our luggage arrived. Since we had a limo waiting for us, I told my wife not to worry, once we got home, I would take our car to pick up the luggage.

We were both exhausted after the long flight, but she was pregnant and needed to rest, so she agreed. Besides, we knew our parents would probably be waiting at our house to hear all about our trip. Sure enough, they were there.

After telling our folks that our luggage was on another flight, I told them to make coffee and I would get donuts on the way back from the airport. Then we could all watch our honeymoon videos together.

What I didn't tell them was that I would make a quick stop on my way to the airport for cocaine. My thinking was that I would snort it later that night when our parents left, after my wife fell asleep.

The moment I held the bag in my hand, everything quickly changed. I was Jonesing so badly for it that I snorted some up my nose the moment it was in my possession.

I made it safely to the airport. After putting the luggage in the car, I drove off. Before I knew it, I pulled the car to the side of the road and did another big line of cocaine. That's when the paranoia kicked in. Not wanting to arouse suspicion in my wife or our parents, I decided to drive around until the high wore off.

Before I knew it, I had snorted it all and needed more, and didn't make it home until 3 days later! That's right. This isn't a typo. I really did say, three days later!!!

As you can imagine, my paranoia and shame had reached levels never before experienced. I kept saying to myself, "What am I going to do?!" But instead of going home to face the music, like any addict worth their salt, I drove to the seediest areas of Philadelphia, to purchase more cocaine.

It was already bad enough going to those places when I wasn't high on drugs. Going there stoned made me even more paranoid. I saw two sunrises and three sunsets on that binge. My father and wife were calling hospitals and jails looking for me. I was so ashamed!!

Finally, when I was out of money, I went home to face the music. Both our parents were there waiting for me! There was no getting out of this one. That was the first red flag her parents saw in me. And it was a very big red flag! If this would have happened before we were married, perhaps there wouldn't have been a wedding...

After the airport nightmare, I settled back into my job. I worked long hours trying to put it all behind me. But nothing changed. Just like before we were married, I would call her saying I would be leaving in an hour or so, when, in reality, I was already finished.

If she knew I was lying, she wasn't saying anything...at least not yet. I tried to enjoy our time together on my nights off but sometimes I would purposely pick a fight with her, just so I could storm out of the house and get high.

SEIZURE TIME

Two months after our honeymoon, my wife and I had an argument and I stormed out of the house. After scoring coke, I went to a friend's house, who just happened to be one of the waitresses at work. I told her my wife and I were arguing and that I needed to vent, and so on and so forth.

She had a young daughter living with her who didn't deserve having me in her house high as a kite or doing lines of cocaine in the bathroom. Though both were unaware of it, it was foolish of me.

After the coke ran out, I needed more. The problem was my inspection stickers on my car were expired, so I asked if I could borrow her car to see my wife for an hour or so. I told her I felt bad about the fight but was afraid to drive my car because of the bad inspection stickers.

"Of course," she said, "no problem."

After another three-day binge, I had a cocaine induced seizure while driving her car. I passed out and drove it into the front of someone's house. Her car was completely totaled.

All I remember was waking up in a hospital, and seeing a Philadelphia policeman rubbing my hands. After asking what happened, and why I was here, he told me I had a cocaine-induced seizure and I crashed into the front of a house. He told me no one was injured. He told me when the medics shot me up with adrenaline I started swinging at the police.

I was freaking out because I didn't remember any of it. I waited for him to say, "Michael Higgins, you are under arrest for such and such charges," but it never happened.

At the very least, I should have received a DUI. He said, "Michael, you're going to be alright. Your wife and your father are on their way to take you first to detox, followed by a 28-day residential rehab program."

On the way to the detox center, my body felt heavy; I was woozy. Three days later I was off to rehab. I was cocaine free for three days. It was early November, and I was starting to feel a little better.

After the airport incident, my relationship with her parents was strained, especially with my mother-in-law. My father, on the other hand, told me not to worry about anything except getting a day clean.

He said, "At this juncture, nothing else matters."

43

So that's what I did. In rehab, I fell more in love with my wife for being so understanding. I put her through so much already. I couldn't wait until visitation day. More importantly, I couldn't wait to go home with her as a new man and husband.

I was excited knowing we were expecting our first child in two months or so. One night I wrote her parents a lengthy and heartfelt letter letting them know I was a terrible husband and son-in-law. I asked them to please forgive me and that I was a changed man. I had no idea what kind of reaction I would get.

Her mother cried when she read the letter.

I got out of rehab early in December. My wife picked me up and we went out to eat. When we got home we were both shocked. When my wife came to pick me up her parents went to our house, put up a Christmas tree, and filled the room with gifts for us. We were stunned. I started crying. That was an awesome day.

I started going to Narcotics Anonymous (N.A.) meetings every day. I lost my job. Once again, another good job with great potential down the toilet. I'd had a good relationship with the owner but now he didn't want to speak to me. And my waitress friend hated my guts. Thankfully, we were able to buy her another car.

With so much going on, I decided not to work for a while. I needed to focus all my attention on my recovery, and on preparing for the birth of our son in just a few short weeks...

THE BIRTH OF OUR FIRST SON

After Christmas and New Year's Eve, which were incredible due to the fact that I was clean and sober for nearly two months, we were increasingly excited for the birth of our son. His due date was January 25th. At that time, by choice, we didn't know if it was a boy or a girl.

Midway through the month of January, the first Gulf war erupted in the Middle East. Aside from going to my daily N.A. meetings and getting the baby room ready, I couldn't stop watching the war coverage on CNN. My eyes were riveted by what they saw. It was fascinating, yet frightening and sobering to see.

Every night before going to bed I got on my knees in front of the crib and thanked God for my life and for the baby soon to be born. This was truly the best time of my life up to that point.

Everyone told me how good I looked and how proud they were of me, including her parents.

Life was good, stable...

On a cold rainy evening in late January, my wife's water broke. As she prepared to go to the hospital I made the necessary calls to family members and friends.

With this being the first grandchild on either side of the family, many family members and friends joined us at the hospital.

On January 31st, after nineteen hours of labor, she gave birth to a son. Up to that point, it was truly the greatest feeling of my life. When my son was born, the nurses let me take him out to the waiting area to introduce him to everyone.

I tried saying, "It's a boy," but burst into tears instead, prompting the nurse to make the announcement for me.

Everyone was overjoyed. Some even cried with me.

The next day I went to a department store to purchase a robe for my wife. An older woman approached me and said, "You just had a baby, didn't you?"

"Yes. How did you know?"

She replied, "Man, you got the walk."

That blew me away. The same day I brought pastries for the nursing staff thanking them for everything they did for us. They replied saying, "No, thank you. Your expressions were priceless."

Things couldn't have been any better; I actually thought I was cured of my cocaine addiction...

FINISHED WITH THE RESTAURANT BUSINESS

When we brought our son home from the hospital, I had a new career waiting for me whenever I was ready to begin. Actually, it was a new business opportunity my twin brother had gotten involved with, with a network marketing company called National Safety Associates (NSA).

After just a few months in business, my brother opened his own office. The energy reverberating in that place was always positive and upbeat. It was exactly what I needed back then. I excelled immediately and started making money practically from day one. I loved going there in the mornings followed by N.A. meetings at night. The rest of the day was spent with my wife and our son.

I quickly became one of the office leaders. My brother put me in charge of collecting desk fees. Full-time reps paid $350 a month for the use of a professional office which included a desk, leadership training, coffee, utilities, and so on.

At that time, I was five months clean. I was honored to be trusted with such a big responsibility. I felt great at this stage...almost invincible.

The next month, as I was collecting desk rents, it happened: instead of paying by check, one of the associates gave me $350.00 in cash. Immediately, the cash in my hand woke up that sleeping tiger inside me. I was off to the races and was nowhere to be found for two days.

When the money and cocaine were gone, it was time to face the music again. My house was full of family members. Everyone was disappointed in me. Again. They reminded me that I had a wife and child to take care of and that I needed to get my act together.

Once again, everything I worked so hard for was gone like that. As great as I had felt for those six months, I couldn't have felt any worse in those two or three days. I felt ashamed being around even my son who always loved me no matter what. The trust I'd built up was gone.

My wife, God bless her, still chose to stand by my side. But many at the office started treating me differently. Not only that, my checks had dwindled to practically nothing in the coming months.

I kept plugging away with my business and going to N.A. meetings but not on a regular basis. My biggest task was trying to shield my cocaine use from everyone else.

When I was out of money, I went to friends saying my car broke down and I needed money for a tow truck. I offered to give them personal checks which would have bounced had they ever been deposited. Most gave me cash with no strings attached.

SEIZURE TIME AGAIN AND AGAIN AND AGAIN

Less than a year after my first cocaine-induced seizure, I went on another binge which lasted several days. Too afraid to go home, I drove hundreds of miles in and around Philadelphia, buying cocaine until the money ran out.

Once again, I woke up in the same hospital not knowing who I was, why I was there, or what I had done this time.

Once again, there was a Philadelphia police officer in my room rubbing my hand saying, "You're going to be alright."

When I finally came to my senses, the kind officer told me I'd had a cocaine-induced seizure and that I hit several parked cars with my car, which happened to be a rental.

He told me witnesses said that after hitting a few cars on one side of the street, I did the same thing on the other side, like a pinball in a pinball machine. The only good thing he said was that I didn't hit or kill anybody. Thank God. Had that happened, I wouldn't have been able to live with myself.

At any rate, the shame I felt was overwhelming.

At this point, my in-laws were totally fed up with me. They'd had enough. From that moment on, I never felt comfortable around them. The trust was gone.

My wife, on the other hand, though she didn't trust me, was still willing to stick it out with me. But only if I agreed to go to daily meetings no matter what. I agreed to her condition, but it was nothing more than a desperate plea on my part.

I loved my wife and wanted to remain married to her, but my addiction was so strong, I couldn't stop. Most times when I was supposed to be at N.A. meetings, I was out looking for cocaine.

It didn't take long for her to realize what I was doing. She knew when I was high just by looking in my eyes. It got to where she drove me to the meetings. When she couldn't, she would drive by to see if my car was there or not.

She was pregnant at the time with our second child and caring for two other babies, our first son and me. She didn't deserve what I had put her through. When our first son was born, I was clean and sober. When our second son was born, I'm quite sure I wasn't.

Our marriage was quite turbulent by this time. My wife worked the night shift from 7 p.m. to 7 a.m. One day before coming home from work, I copped some coke knowing she would be at work. I did this often hoping I would have enough to last through the night.

But on this particular night, I ran out and needed more. I left the kids at home as they slept in their beds, then drove 30-minutes each way for more cocaine.

You would think once would be enough, but my addiction was so bad that I did it on a few occasions. But I was always back home before the kids woke or my wife got home from work.

But not this night…

On the way home, I kept telling myself there was no way I'd make it home before my wife. I drove around the neighborhood several times wondering if she was home or not. Since she always parked her car in the garage, I had no way of knowing.

Paranoia continued to snake through me, to the extent that I drove around the city several hours more, before finally deciding to go home to face my wife. When I arrived, my in-laws were there. On the living room table were the Playboy and Hustler magazines I hid under the couch, along with the pornography tapes I'd left in the VCR. I was mortified.

I was told when my wife walked in the house, the kids were crying in their cribs with wet diapers. Thank God nothing ever happened to the children when I left them home alone!

Had I been in my right mind, none of this would have ever happened. But I was a full-blown drug addict, and everyone knew it.

By this time my in-laws had completely written me off. Not surprisingly, my wife wasn't too far behind her parents. Even this wasn't enough to pull me away from the stronghold cocaine had on my life. If anything, it only got worse.

When I wasn't working but needed money for drugs, I'd drive to local WaWa convenience stores saying I was a regular customer and that my car broke down and the tow truck driver only accepted cash. The solution? I needed them to cash my personal checks, which I knew would only bounce once deposited.

Of course, I knew writing bad checks was a felony, but I didn't care; my cocaine addiction was so strong that nothing else mattered to me, including committing possible felonies. All I wanted, needed, was more cocaine! There was little difference between me and a heroin addict knowing the needle he would stick in his arm might kill him or give him AIDS or something. It mattered not...

Most stores were willing to cash checks for fifty dollars, which went straight up my nose. On this regrettable day, I must have gone to five different stores. I could only imagine how I looked by the fourth or fifth one.

When I left the last convenience store, I saw a cop car in the parking lot. I didn't know it yet, but the police officer was there for me. As I drove away, he followed me a while before finally pulling me over.

After telling me I was under arrest for writing bad checks and that I would be going away for a long time, he placed me in handcuffs, put me in the back of the squad car and drove me to the Bensalem Police Department Building.

On the way there, the officer asked what I was doing with the money. Looking at me in his rear-view mirror, he said, "Never mind, I can see it in your eyes."

Miraculously, he didn't take me into custody. Instead, he asked me for a contact number, so I gave him my twin brother's number.

The last thing I wanted was to give him my wife's number. I remember thinking my brother would be more understanding of the situation than her. Sure enough, he picked me up at the police department and told me how lucky I was that they weren't pressing charges against me.

Once again, it was off to rehab. My wife didn't visit me nearly as much this time. At this point, her parents constantly pressured her to leave me for good. She was still sticking with me, but she wanted me to move out until I got my act together.

So, I moved in with my brother and started going to meetings on a daily basis. I would see her and the kids a couple times a week. She lived in Philly and I now lived in New Jersey.

I started working in the restaurant business again. This was the beginning of the end of my marriage. I was still lying to her all the time but now she knew better.

In no time, I became a burden to my brother and his girlfriend, so I left my brother's place and moved into a roach-infested, fleabag motel getting high all the time.

Several months later, as I was lying in bed stoned out of my head, I heard a loud knock on the door. I nearly jumped out of my skin. I truly thought it was the cops coming to arrest me. I couldn't look out the window because they would see me.

The loud knocking continued. I had no choice but to answer the door. It wasn't the police. I was being served divorce papers. I was shaking like a leaf in front of this man. I was so stoned and didn't know how they had found me there.

I'll never forget how I felt after signing the papers. Suddenly accountable to no one, it felt like all hope was lost...

At this point in my life, I hadn't been to an N.A. meeting in many months. I had no plans of ever going again. I also stopped going to church on Sunday. There aren't too many things worse than the hopeless feeling of not caring anymore.

Several months later, after another three-day binge, I suffered another cocaine-induced seizure. I ended up in a different hospital outside of Philadelphia this time. When I came out of my stupor, the doctor told me what happened. I admitted to having used cocaine the night before. Because of my honesty, he said there would be no need to draw blood from my veins.

The most humiliating thing was calling my brother to come get me again. I felt even lower than the last time, if you can believe that?

There would be no more meetings and no more rehabs, just hopelessness and despair. I was doing more cocaine now than ever before. So much more! I was like a test rat always in need of the family-shredding white powdery substance!

On one particular binge, I thought I was going to be killed. I drove to a dangerous neighborhood in Philadelphia looking for cocaine. It was mid-afternoon, and I was wired for sound. I always felt safer buying cocaine at night, so being in broad daylight made me feel all the more paranoid.

Anyway, there were no close parking spots, so I was forced to park on another street. There was a baseball field with a huge chain link fence that took up the entire city block. I saw my dealer on the other street through the chain link fence.

After making the exchange with my dealer, I walked back to my car; out of nowhere came three Hispanic dudes. They jumped out of their car and put a knife to my throat. They took my wallet, car keys, and my money. They were laughing at me and harassing me.

My drug dealer noticed and came to my rescue. "Give back everything you took from him! Everything," he yelled. Imagine that? The man who just sold me a substance that could potentially kill me, had just possibly saved my life.

Anyway, when the three thugs saw him, they looked like they just saw a ghost. Without protest, they did as they were instructed, they got in their car and drove off.

I nodded my head at him. He nodded back. I got into my car and drove off. I believe those dudes would have killed me had it not been for him. Needless to say, I was shaken by the experience, but it didn't stop me.

Several months later, after another three-day binge, I suffered another cocaine-induced seizure (my fourth one). By this time, I had moved back with my twin brother and his "now" wife and children. He let me borrow his car to go to work. After work, I was at a local casino because I didn't want to go back to my brother's house stoned.

As I was leaving the casino I backed into a pole while I was having the seizure. I remember a man yelling at me, "Michael! Michael! Michael!" He was clapping his hands loudly. It woke me up but as soon as they put me in the ambulance I passed out again.

When I woke in the hospital the doctor was in the room—a female this time. After asking how I felt, I told her I felt terrible because I knew why I was there.

She told me I was lucky to be alive.

In my mind, I didn't think so; I just wanted to die. After performing an M.R.I. on my brain, she shocked me by saying she didn't believe I had seizures at all, as alleged. I insisted that the other hospitals had said I had cocaine-induced seizures.

She asked, "Did you urinate in your pants those other times?"

I told her I didn't think so.

She pointed her finger upward and said, "I think someone above is trying to get your attention!"

It gave me goose bumps at the time, but even her sobering words didn't stop me from using cocaine...

NO MORE FAITH

I soon left my brother's house and moved into a motel room. I had become robotlike with only one command to obey: score more cocaine. I'm sure I looked like the walking dead.

My life had become entirely predictable. It was the same thing every day. My nose was so bad from snorting cocaine that I constantly needed tissues. I could hardly smell anything at all. It got so bad that even snorting cocaine was difficult.

The motel I was living in was in the suburbs, which meant I had to drive to the city every night to feed my addiction. If it meant cutting corners at work to get out sooner, so be it. This mindset, not to mention that I was calling out of work too much, ended up costing me a few jobs. This *never* happened before my addiction! I went from being one of the best employees to mediocre at best in no time.

Anyway, that New Year's Eve, I drove to the city for cocaine. I can still remember how proud I felt for achieving my warped goal, which was to arrive there before midnight, only to learn my regular drug dealers weren't there. As they rang in the New Year with family and friends, all I wanted was to get high.

When I got out of the car, a man put a gun to my head and said, "Give me all your money."

I took the money out of my pocket and gave it to him.

He then said, "You better dig deeper, man."

I told him it was all I had. I said, "Take my car if you want but I have no more money."

He then said, "Get in your car now and drive away."

As soon as I got in my car and started it up, he shot a bullet in the air. How bizarre. I started off the new year with a gun to my head!

I was trembling as I drove away, but it I got over it rather quickly because I didn't care anymore. Why should I?

I'd lost my marriage, my children, most of my family, I had no real home to live in, and every dollar I earned or stole went straight up my nose.

The thought of a bullet ripping through my head was almost comforting! It was the same crazy routine every day. I would often question God often, "Why is this happening to me? I'm a good guy! I can't understand this."

My addiction was so bad that I had no business driving a car let alone working a job and dealing with customers. I seldom slept. I was truly a lost soul with no hope in sight. I had been turned into a lying, thieving, scheming, abandoning, untrustworthy, adulterer.

The worse part was that I accepted this unscrupulous lifestyle.

My brother would occasionally come in to eat where I worked with his friends. One man, a good friend named Charles, always asked if he could pray for me. I would always say yes, and he would lay his hands on me and pray right there in the restaurant.

Out of sheer embarrassment, instead of closing my eyes, I surveyed the restaurant to see who was staring at us.

When he finished praying for me he would often say, "Faith the size of a mustard seed can move mountains."

I had no idea what he was talking about, but I always thanked him for praying for me. Even after all that, nothing ever seemed to change. When they left, it was always back to business.

This went on for many years.

My family kept waiting for a call from the coroner.

BUT GOD...

PART THREE:

MY

LIFE

AFTER

COCAINE

MY HALLELUJAH MOMENT

A few years before Jesus delivered me from my cocaine addiction, I had genuinely received Him as my Lord and Savior. I was on the road with my twin brother and even went to church with him.

After hearing a sermon which I believe was preached just for me, the pastor did an altar call. With tears flowing down my cheeks, I repented of my sins and trusted in Christ as Lord and Savior.

I had the most amazing feeling inside. It was unlike anything I'd ever encountered before.

For the first time in my life, I felt the Spirit of God living inside me. I felt safe. I started seeing changes in my life that could only be attributed to the Holy Spirit living inside me. One of those changes was that I started listening to Christian music. And being on the road so much with my brother and his wife forced me to behave.

The problem was that I was still addicted to cocaine. And this meant I wasn't walking with Jesus like I should have been. Upon returning from those road trips, instead of reading the Bible or going to church, it was off to the races for me. It shames me to confess that even after receiving Jesus as Lord and Savior, I still did thousands and thousands of dollars worth of cocaine.

Even though I knew I was saved, which meant I had eternal assurance, it didn't always feel that way. In fact, I often felt utterly hopeless because of the way I was living my life, especially after what Jesus did on the cross for me. To say I was wracked with guilt and shame would be putting it mildly. Despite all that, the Lord kept forgiving me and was slowly transforming me from the inside out, even if it didn't appear that way. Thank you, Lord!

Now for my Hallelujah Moment—chains that had all but suffocated the life out of me were about to be broken! All throughout my addiction years, I often argued with my wife and family members. Most of the arguments were drug related, but not all of them.

Even so, if ever I tried defending myself, I was always told I was a drug addict and that I knew nothing. This was something I had to live with for a very long time. Whether I was right or wrong, they always made one thing crystal clear to me: I was a drug addict.

One day my brother and I were having an argument. About what? I don't remember. However, after all was said and done, I heard him say those familiar words again, "What do you know? You're a drug addict!"

I paused a moment and said, "Look into my eyes. I haven't done cocaine in months." So many times in the past I would lie and say I wasn't high on cocaine when I really was. But not that time. I truly was cocaine free, and the words I spoke couldn't come close to describing how I felt.

Can I get a HALLELUJAH?!

Just like that, I no longer had the urge to use cocaine! Jesus took it away just like that, in the blink of an eye. I know it sounds crazy, but it's true. I wasn't going to church, nor going to meetings of any kind; it just happened!

I immediately recognized the miracle. It was JESUS!

Again, can I get a HALLELUJAH?!

Think about it, I tried everything at one time or another. Two detox programs, three drug rehabs, frequent counseling, AA meetings, NA meetings, CA meetings. Many were ready and willing to do anything to help me, yet nothing worked.

A couple years before I was delivered from my cocaine addiction, my father told me he had cancer. Upon hearing this, I was devastated and decided to help my mother take care of him to the best of my ability. When I wasn't working, I spent most of my time at their house. I was still battling my cocaine addiction at that time.

Aside from my twin brother, the person who was most willing to help me back then was my father. With many years of sobriety under his belt, he did all he could to help me, but I still wasn't ready.

My father knew how badly I was struggling. Before he died he said, "Michael, look into my eyes. I can honestly tell you I haven't had a drink or a cigarette in twenty-seven years."

I nodded my head wondering how in the world he did it? Today it's crystal clear to me. Thank You, Jesus.

I only wish he was still alive to see me now!

Like I said earlier, in the case of me and my father, the fruit didn't fall far from the tree. I praise God for that.

Looking back, as I write this, maybe just maybe, Jesus delivered me from cocaine at that precise time because of my obedience in taking care of my father when he needed me.

One day I will know...

At any rate, the fog was clearing and, with a heart full of joy and gratitude, I couldn't stop thanking Jesus for changing my life. But due to the many lies I'd told in the past, who would believe me? I'm pretty sure my brother didn't, but could you blame him?

My father used to tell me the acronym of time was:

This

I

Must

Earn

In short: I knew it would take more than just words for my family and friends to see the miraculous change in me. Even if they couldn't see it yet, I felt something inside that I hadn't had in a very long time—peace of mind.

I was comforted by John 8:36 (NLT) which states, "So if the Son sets you free, you are truly free."

To this day, I don't know the exact day when Jesus set me free from my cocaine addiction. All that matters is that He did.

Luke 15:1-7 ESV The Parable of the Lost Sheep says: 1) Now the tax collectors and sinners were all drawing near to hear Him. 2) And the Pharisees and the scribes grumbled, saying, "This man receives sinners and eats with them." 3) So he told them this parable: 4) What man of you, having a hundred sheep, if he has lost one of them, does not leave the ninety-nine in the open country, and go after the one that is lost, until he finds it? 5) And when he has found it, he lays it on his shoulders, rejoicing. 6) And when he comes home, he calls together his friends and his neighbors, saying to them, "Rejoice with me, for I have found my sheep that was lost." 7) Just so, I tell you, there will be more joy in heaven over one sinner who repents than over ninety-nine righteous persons who need no repentance."

I can only imagine how many others have been blessed by that parable, but as far as I'm concerned it was written just for me.

Thank You, Jesus! Thank You, Jesus! Thank You, Jesus!

FAITH THE SIZE OF A MUSTARD SEED

Like I said earlier, many people prayed for me during this dark period of my life. I'm eternally grateful to each of them.

My twin brother, Patrick, whom I put through a lot, is at the very top of the list. He didn't pray for me for twenty days, or twenty weeks, or twenty months, he prayed for more than twenty years for my deliverance from cocaine and that I would surrender my life to Christ Jesus. Of all the things he did for me, by far, his prayers far outweighed everything else. Thank you, bro!

Our good friend Charles Culmer also prayed for me without ceasing. He's the one who would lay hands on me at the restaurants I worked at saying, "Faith the size of a mustard seed can move mountains."

I never knew what that meant back then. Now I do.

Thank you, Charles...

I now see how God had answered their prayers. Looking back, at any given time during my cocaine addiction years, I could have had a heart attack and died. Believe me when I say, my heart was doing things it wasn't supposed to do. I eventually got used to it, but some nights were especially terrifying for me.

I remember one time my heart raced so wildly in my chest, it felt like something had shifted inside me. I was frightened. It was

59

at that time that I pleaded with God saying, "Please don't take me now. I'm not ready to meet You."

I can't recall the exact day I uttered those words skyward, but I believe that's when my "faith the size of a mustard seed moment" came to fruition. In God's perfect will and timing, He moved that mountain in front of me called cocaine.

Just like that...poof...it was gone!

For more than 20 years, I was a slave to that mountain. I couldn't get over or around it, no matter how hard I tried. It would tell me to jump and I would say, "How high?" Not anymore!

Now I only jump for Jesus! Matthew 17:20 (NLT) says, "You don't have enough faith,' Jesus told them. 'I tell you the truth, if you had faith even as small as a mustard seed, you could say to this mountain, 'Move from here to there,' and it would move. Nothing would be impossible."

I believe with all my heart that God can move mountains in your life too, to get you where He wants you to be.

It's just a matter of faith.

Question is: Do you have faith the size of a mustard seed?

If so, God can do exactly for you what He did for me.

MOVING TO FLORIDA...

In 2008, my brother and I moved to Florida for a business venture. I was leaving a lot of baggage and problems in Pennsylvania knowing there was nothing I could do about them at this juncture.

I decided I would clear the slate and I went with the hope that one day, with God's help, I'd be able to make things right with the people I hurt. His will be done.

Before we left I said to myself, "When I get to Florida, for the first time in my life, I will put my complete faith in Jesus." I truly meant it. I was so grateful I wasn't using cocaine anymore and I was grateful to be alive!

In addition, I also decided from now on to make myself available for Jesus to use me any way He wished.

We loaded everything we had into a U-Haul truck and left the Keystone State for the Sunshine State. What a long day that was! It took seven or eight hours just to load the moving truck. We were already exhausted, but we were determined to leave that day.

We got on I-95 southbound and drove straight thru the night. With the plan in motion, I started getting excited about having a business and not having to work in a restaurant ever again.

In no time, the business venture went under. This was not a good thing. You can probably remember the horrible financial collapse of 2008. Now this? I was counting on never working in the restaurant business again and my left knee loved the sound of that.

Who knew this would happen? Everything we planned and worked for was gone. We were a couple of months into a one-year lease on a very expensive apartment with no money coming in.

So, it was off to find another restaurant job. Praise God I found one rather quickly at a local eatery.

Unfortunately, after a few months on the job, I fell and broke my wrist. I didn't even know it was broken until several hours later. I was working a double shift that day. During the dinner shift, I was tending bar. When someone ordered a beer, I couldn't even open the bottle.

My manager told me to go to the hospital and once there they told me my wrist was broken. This was a terrible time for this to happen. My first few months in Florida were no better than they were in Pennsylvania. It was as if Satan was trying to pull me back into the world I had just been delivered from.

When the cast was removed a few months later, I was told it wasn't healing correctly and I needed to have surgery.

Things were very tight financially speaking but my faith in God was still intact. I went to church every week and truly loved it. Eager to become a better person, I joined many groups and was learning how to live more like Jesus.

For the first time in my life, I was finally hanging out with the right crowd. There is an old saying that states, "You can either hang with the turkeys or fly with the eagles."

I was starting to fly with the eagles.

61

IF YOU DON'T HAVE A BIBLE,
TAKE ONE HOME WITH YOU

Because of my serious financial struggles, I worried so much that I couldn't sleep most nights. But I was always energized on Sunday because I knew I would be going to church. It used to be football day for me, but not anymore. Don't get me wrong, I still watched football games on Sunday, but it was no longer a top priority.

One Sunday at church, Pastor David Uth was teaching from the book of Psalms. Near the end of his sermon, he said, "If anyone here doesn't have a Bible, take the one in front of you." I did just that.

Being so new to all this, I had no idea what the book of Psalms was, but since Pastor had read from it, I decided to start there.

It figures...the longest book in the Bible. Up to that time, I wasn't a reader. But God quickly changed all that. After finishing the book of Psalms, I moved on to the book of Proverbs.

As I neared the end of Proverbs, someone told me Jesus could be found in the book of Matthew. That's what I read next.

Suddenly, all I wanted to do was read the Word. The more I read it, the more I learned how I was supposed to live my life. I loved the man I was becoming, even despite my financial woes.

When I told a good friend from my church, a man named Gary Haskell, that I was reading the Gospel of Matthew, so I could learn more about the life of Jesus, he was happy to hear that. I told him I was confused by the many things Jesus did to fulfill certain scriptures or prophecies, and wanted to know how I could know which scripture or prophet Matthew was referring to?

Gary explained that if I had a study Bible, it would help me to better connect the dots, so to speak. He then purchased one for me and challenged me to read it from cover to cover, from Genesis to

Revelation. By so doing, he assured me I would find answers to all my questions.

That's exactly what I did. Though this new study Bible was quite intimidating at first—after all it was twice the size of my Bible—I started reading it every day and asking God to give me more understanding.

In addition, I vowed to Him that no matter how far-fetched His Word might seem—Noah living to be 950 years old, for example—instead of scratching my head in utter confusion, I would believe every little, itty bitty word of it. I figured it was the least I could do after He delivered me from my cocaine addiction.

Before you knew it, I was believing more and doubting less.

On December 25th 2009 (Christmas Day), I finished reading the Bible all the way through. What a journey it was! What a day to finish it! I felt so blessed. The Holy Spirit was really moving in me.

It was one of the greatest sensations of my life. I realized after reading the Bible that it truly is God's love letter for humanity.

Not only that, it's the only Book ever written that when you open it up, the author shows up! Every time!

Could you imagine reading a crazy demonic secular book and having its author show up? No, thank you! I'd rather have the King of the Universe show up and guide my steps.

The first time through the Bible, some of the words and verses stung quite a bit. They accused and convicted me, and I quickly realized that if I were living in the Old Testament days, I would have been stoned to death at a very early age.

Thank You, Jesus, for your limitless mercy and grace!

The second time through the Bible, I highlighted key passages that really spoke to me. This time I finished reading it on Easter Sunday! Amazing! Think about it: the first time I finished was on the celebration of Jesus' birth and the second time was on His resurrection. How cool is that?!

I now read the Bible from cover to cover once a year. I recommend you do the same for yourself. By so doing, like me, you will learn that, while it's true the life of Jesus is recorded in the book of Matthew—and the three other Gospels—the more you read and study the Word, you will come to see that He is in every other book in the Bible as well, from Genesis to Revelation.

I wish to thank Pastor Uth and Gary Haskell for providing me with my first Bible and study Bible. Much of my spiritual growth can be attributed to the seeds you planted in me when I was still a babe in Christ. God bless you both.

MATTHEW 25:31-46—THE FINAL JUDGMENT

The one Bible passage that spoke to me louder than the others was Matthew 25:31-46. The sub-title was The Final Judgment. And seeing that the letters were red in color, I knew Jesus had spoken those words. I took it very seriously.

It said, [31]"When the Son of Man comes in his glory, and all the angels with him, then he will sit on his glorious throne. [32] Before him will be gathered all the nations, and he will separate people one from another as a shepherd separates the sheep from the goats. [33] And he will place the sheep on his right, but the goats on the left.

[34] Then the King will say to those on his right, 'Come, you who are blessed by my Father, inherit the kingdom prepared for you from the foundation of the world. [35] For I was hungry and you gave me food, I was thirsty and you gave me drink, I was a stranger and you welcomed me, [36] I was naked and you clothed me, I was sick and you visited me, I was in prison and you came to me.'

[37] Then the righteous will answer him, saying, 'Lord, when did we see you hungry and feed you, or thirsty and give you drink? [38] And when did we see you a stranger and welcome you, or naked and clothe you? [39] And when did we see you sick or in prison and visit you?' [40] And the King will answer them, 'Truly, I say to you, as you did it to one of the least of these my brothers, you did it to me.'

[41]"Then he will say to those on his left, 'Depart from me, you cursed, into the eternal fire prepared for the devil and his angels. [42] For I was hungry and you gave me no food, I was thirsty and you gave me no drink, [43] I was a stranger and you did not welcome me,

naked and you did not clothe me, sick and in prison and you did not visit me.'

[44] Then they also will answer, saying, 'Lord, when did we see you hungry or thirsty or a stranger or naked or sick or in prison, and did not minister to you?' [45] Then he will answer them, saying, 'Truly, I say to you, as you did not do it to one of the least of these, you did not do it to me.' [46] And these will go away into eternal punishment, but the righteous into eternal life."

This passage completely changed my life and ultimately helped define my future feeding ministry. To reiterate what Jesus said, "I was hungry and you either fed me or you did not feed me. I was thirsty, and you gave me a drink, or you did not. I was naked and you either clothed me or you did not. I was in prison and you visited me or you did not. I was a stranger and you welcomed me, or you did not. I was sick, and you visited me, or you did not."

After reading this I said, "I can do these things."

But if I did, they had to be done in love. After all, Jesus said the greatest commandment is to: "Love the Lord your God with all your heart, soul, mind and strength." The second commandment is: "Love your neighbor as you love yourself." We cannot be true Christians if we do not obey these two commandments. If we master these two, we master them all. Then Jesus gave a new commandment to his disciples. He said, "Love one another as I have loved you."

All three commandments written above start with the word *love*. They are commandments, not suggestions. Love is an action word. It's the evidence of our faith in Jesus. Nuff said!

ONE STEP FORWARD, TWO STEPS BACK

As I was faithfully going to church and growing in the Lord I seemed to be getting attacked from everywhere. Within a couple of months, the two restaurants at which I had two part-time jobs both closed due to the economy.

In Orlando, we depend on tourists to keep businesses going. But they simply weren't coming! This couldn't have happened at a worse time for me. I was barely getting by. Now this?

I had to find another job, and fast. Normally, with all my experience in the restaurant industry, finding a job was never a problem. I applied everywhere. Most people said I was exactly what they were looking for, but they couldn't hire me because of the sagging economy.

I was so discouraged and frightened of being thrown out on the streets. My head was spinning again, which was always a bad place for me to be. Even so, for the first time in my life, I was going through my problems instead of around them. Another miracle.

During this time, I volunteered at my church on Wednesday nights serving food at our weekly church dinner. I was fed nutritious meals after each serving and also took platters home with me. This was a major blessing considering my critical situation.

The place I lived in didn't play games. If your rent wasn't paid on time, they would immediately start the eviction process. It happened this particular month. We were 10 days behind on the rent, so they put a sheriff's notice on our front door saying we had 24 hours to vacate the premises.

The 'old' Michael, in his prideful nature, would never ask for help but this time, out of desperation, I did. Thankfully, a friend at church bailed us out. (If you are reading this book, you know who you are, and I can't thank you enough.)

That was such a huge weight off my shoulders, but it was nothing more than a band aid until the next month.

My friend, Brian, called me from Philly, and after telling him of my situation, he told me there was no recession at the restaurant where I used to work. He said they would love to have me back. After telling my mother about the situation, she said I could stay with her for as long as I needed. I was going a thousand miles north to work so I didn't get evicted in Florida.

It made me very sad, mainly because I loved my church and was already missing it before I even drove one mile. I went to take a nap before the long drive. As I started to doze off, the phone rang. It was a place called Pizza Fusion. They wanted me to come in for an interview.

I prayed, "Lord, let this job keep me here in Florida."

After the interview, I calculated in my head that it would be just enough money to keep me there. My sadness turned to instant joy! Thank You, Jesus! What a feeling! I could remain in Florida and continue going to my home church!

Another miracle for me was my work schedule. Normally, I would ask for Sundays and Mondays off for football season. At my new job I asked for Sundays and Wednesdays off, so I could go to church and continue volunteering at the Wednesday night dinners. They agreed to my wishes.

That's what I call spiritual growth! Are you noticing all these "little" miracles happening?

ALL I WANT TO DO IS SERVE

With things slowly but steadily settling into place, I joined several classes at church. One class was focused on personal ministry. For four or five weeks (I forget exactly how many), we discussed volunteering our time and were provided with names and numbers of local ministries in need of assistance.

One ministry that immediately caught my attention was the Good News Prison Ministry. Knowing most men in prison were there because of drugs—either buying or selling—I very easily could have been sitting in prison right along with them.

The only difference between me and them is that I never got caught. I truly believed this was where God wanted me."

With that in mind, I filled out all the necessary paperwork and was told I would receive an answer within a few weeks, either way.

I had a full-time job that barely paid the bills, but I was still grateful for my new life. In addition to that, I was going to church (and wanting to be there) and volunteering on a weekly basis.

I had been volunteering at the church for several months by this time, and I truly loved it. But my new desire was to go deep into the trenches and do some serious bragging about what Jesus did in my life. Prison ministry would allow me to do just that.

Talk about being in the trenches! I greatly anticipated hearing from them. Every Wednesday while volunteering at church I would tell myself, "This is the week the prison ministry people will call me."

Several weeks went by and I had yet to hear from them. This did not upset me at the time. I would tell myself, "Perhaps next week."

But as the weeks passed, I found myself growing increasingly disappointed. It's not like I had applied to the secret service for a job protecting the President; all I wanted was to comfort many in prison by sharing the Word of God with them.

The week before the personal ministries course ended, we were advised that we would have individual coaches assigned to us the following week. This was my first introduction to Gary Haskell, the man who gave me the study Bible I mentioned earlier.

On the evening I was scheduled to meet him, he called me. His voice was raspy; he almost sounded like he was in the mafia.

When I answered the phone, he said, "This is Gary Haskell. I'll be your personal ministry coach tonight. I'm calling to make sure that you'll be there, so you don't waste my time."

After assuring him that I would be there, I showered and was out the door.

The instant I met Gary, I liked him. I think I told him most of my life in the first half hour we were together. I'm sure he thought I was crazy at first. Even so, he stuck with me from the get-go.

The Lord used Gary during this uncertain time of my life in a very powerful and gracious way.

As the weeks passed, we developed a solid friendship. I felt comfortable telling him anything that was on my mind; and I do mean anything!

Every week he would ask if I'd heard anything from the prison ministry people. I would shake my head no—no phone call, email or letter...nothing. I'm sure he saw the disappointment on my face. In short: he knew I was frustrated.

Knowing how badly I wanted to volunteer my time with them, Gary politely suggested that maybe prison ministry wasn't where God wanted me at that time and perhaps He had other plans for me. I wasn't happy with this advice, but I took it and kept on volunteering at the Wednesday night supper.

MY NEW HIGH

A few weeks later I got a clear-cut message placed on my heart by the Lord himself. I was to get lunch bags and write JESUS LOVES YOU on them, fill them with a sandwich, a snack, bag of chips, and a drink, and go tell my "Jesus story" to the homeless in Orlando. I had zero dollars to do this, but I did it anyway. You want to know why? Because I don't use cocaine anymore!!!

It was on a Wednesday in 2009 that I decided to do this. Since Wednesday was my day off from work, and the day I volunteered at the church serving dinners, it was a no-brainer decision.

This was the day the Lord had made available for me to serve Him. I called my mother on the phone and I told her what God had placed on my heart. After I explained it to her, I asked her what she thought, and she said she thought it was a good thing. That really meant a lot to me. I thought she would think I was nuts, like others did, mostly because of my gloomy financial situation.

After I had her blessing, I talked to two women from church and they said they wanted to help put the plan into action.

When the girls from my Starting Point class came over, we cranked up the Christian music, made 25 lunches, and left for downtown Orlando, not knowing where the homeless were.

69

A man told us of a place called Lake Eola. I'd never heard of it before, that's where we went. As we were driving there, we noticed a man walking along I-4. We pulled over to see if he was okay. He said he was hot and thirsty and needed a ride to Daytona Beach.

We told him we were going as far as Lake Eola and offered to take him there. He said it would be a big help. When he got in the car, we gave him something cold to drink and asked if he was hungry.

He shared with us that he had spent the last two nights in jail and didn't eat much there. We gave him a lunch and he scarfed it down, so we gave him another. He was truly grateful for the food. I know it sounds crazy picking up a complete stranger, and I don't recommend anyone doing that in today's uncertain climate, but, again, something told us to do it. He seemed friendly enough.

We explained why we were going to Lake Eola and he, too, assured us that we'd find many homeless people there. We dropped him off before our exit and again he gave us a big "thank you."

We told him Jesus loves him.

He was the second person to tell me that we would find homeless folks at Lake Eola. Needless to say, I was eager to get there.

When we arrived at the park, we saw homeless people everywhere. All the lunches were gone within minutes!

We said, "Jesus loves you" to every man or woman we handed out lunches to. They were so grateful for the food.

As for me personally, I was overwhelmed with emotion and could barely contain myself. I said, "Thank you for this feeling, Jesus!"

A few seconds later, a woman with no teeth came up to me with a big smile saying, "I heard you're giving out lunches to the homeless."

We had to tell her they were already gone. It truly broke my heart, but she told us to keep up the good work.

That was the moment I decided I would make fifty lunches the following week and each week after that, no matter what.

As I was walking back to the car to go home, it dawned on me that this was the cocaine high I'd been chasing for twenty plus years! I felt so good that I probably could have flown home without an airplane!

All week long I was on this amazing high, and couldn't wait for next Wednesday to arrive, so I could feed the homeless again. I very much felt like a kid waiting for Christmas to get here.

On that day, I cranked up Z88.3—our local Christian radio station in Orlando—and made 50 lunches. Every bag had JESUS LOVES YOU written on them. There's nothing like listening to Christian music while making lunches for the homeless—talk about worship! If you don't believe it, try it.

Once I was finished, I loaded the car with the lunch bags and drove 25 miles to Lake Eola, Z88.3 blaring through my car speakers the whole way. The way I felt it was as if the Holy Spirit was doing joyous backflips inside me.

When I arrived at the park, it was different this time. Whereas the homeless were everywhere the week before, I had to go in search of them this time. I walked around the lake and saw many passed out on the grass, perhaps drunk from alcohol or high on drugs.

I gently tapped them on the shoulder asking if they were hungry. Many were startled, as if I was the police.

After assuring them that I only wanted to feed them, they were relieved and gratefully took the lunches. For those who were coherent, I told them how Jesus broke the chains of a 20-year cocaine addiction and that Jesus was able and that He loved them.

For those who didn't wake after being tapped on the shoulder, I left a bagged lunch for them for when they woke up.

After circling the lake and seeing many sitting up eating their lunches, it blew my mind how something so simple could bring so much joy to them. True joy!

Another thing that was different from the first feeding was that I had quit smoking cigarettes. I haven't had one since, praise God! Think about it, when I woke in the morning the first thing I would do is have a cigarette. When I woke up at night to use the restroom I would have a smoke. Before going to bed, I'd light up.

I probably smoked a cigarette every 10-15 minutes every single day. This continued even after I was delivered from cocaine! I tried many times to quit smoking, but I always went back to it.

Just like with my cocaine addiction, Jesus broke the chains of a 30-year cigarette addiction! Another miracle! I had to fill that void with something—that something was Jesus!!!

SACRIFICES PLEASING TO GOD

For the first two years, I pretty much funded the homeless feedings out of my own pocket. There were times when I didn't think I would have enough money for the next feeding. I even thought about feeding bi-weekly to save money. But then something awesome would happen at the lake and I would erase that thought from my mind. I would call the utility companies to make partial payments to ensure that I had enough money to make the lunches.

I worked long hours at the restaurant and every Tuesday evening after work I would go to Walmart to buy the food for Wednesday.

To this day, I still make the sandwiches just before driving to the lake, or any other place, so they are still fresh when received. Some of the people we feed have told us they often get sandwiches from other people and ministries that are two- or three-days old.

But not from me!

Anyway, one day when I was driving to work something awesome happened. I was on Interstate 4 getting ready to exit, when my engine suddenly died. The only thing I could think as I coasted to the red light was that I wouldn't cause a traffic jam. I noticed a left-turn lane, a right-turn lane, and just enough space in between both where I could park without stopping the steady flow of traffic.

Out of nowhere, three men came along and started pushing my car to a gas station less than a tenth of a mile away. I had no idea who they were, but I was extremely grateful.

When we got to the gas station, I got out of my car and assumed they were all homeless. I said, "Thank you, gentlemen, from the bottom of my heart, but I have no money to give you."

One of them pointed his finger at me and said, "Don't worry about it, man. You feed me down at the lake."

Wow!!! Unbelievable!!! My mind was blown, especially since it happened nowhere near Lake Eola.

I shook their hands and thanked them again, then called coworkers for a ride. As I was making calls, one of the men who was very drunk kept talking to me. I told him I would be happy to talk to him after I found a ride to work, but he kept interrupting.

He kept saying, "I'm going crazy, man. I'm going crazy," over and over again. I was opening up the restaurant, so I really needed to concentrate on getting a ride.

Finally, one of the cooks answered and said he would pick me up in a half hour. When I hung up I asked the man why he was going crazy. He said he was drunk and he had to make a change in his life. I knew what he was talking about. I told him what Jesus did for me and that only He can break the chains of addiction.

Seeing a Bible on the passenger front seat in my car, he asked if he could have it.

I told him it was very special to me because my pastor said a while back, "If you don't have your own Bible take the one in front of you."

This was the one I took from the pew rack that Sunday. This Bible meant everything to me and I let him know that.

I said, "If I give it to you, are you going to read it?"

He said, "Yes, sir, I will."

I said, "Okay, take it and cherish it."

73

He said he would and asked me where he should start reading.

I told him, "Because of what your friend said about me feeding him at the lake, read Matthew 25:31-46. When I read this, it changed my life."

Then I encouraged him to read all of Matthew, Mark, Luke, and John, for starters. He said he would do just that. He thanked me for giving him my special Bible.

I told him every answer to every question could be found in there. By this time, his two friends were nowhere to be found. Then, he disappeared too.

Fifteen minutes later Zac, my coworker, arrived. On our way to work, I saw the man I just gave the Bible to sitting at a bus stop reading it. Hallelujah!!!

I said, "Look, Zac! That's the man I was just telling you about!"

Even though I had no idea how much it was going to cost to fix my car, nothing was going to bother me that day.

Hebrews 13:2 ESV says, "Do not neglect to show hospitality to strangers, for thereby some have entertained angels unawares."

Like I said, these guys came out of nowhere. I honestly don't know if I ever saw them again, but the one who pointed his finger at me and said, "Don't worry about it, man. You feed me at the lake," makes me think of this passage. Maybe, just maybe!

At the time, what seemed like many great sacrifices to me, were merely grains of sand compared to the blessings I received as a result of my obedience to what God had called me to do.

MY WORK PLACE

What can I say about my work place, Pizza Fusion? These were the very people who called me months ago while I was in bed resting and dreading that return trip to Philadelphia. Who knows what I would be doing now had I gone back to Philly!

Because of Pizza Fusion, I was able to remain in Orlando and keep growing at my church and start my ministry. That one phone call changed everything. Thank you, Jesus!

Just about everyone in the restaurant, from the owners on down, in one way or another had something to do with my ministry. My passion for Jesus was contagious! I was in love with and on fire for Jesus and they all knew it.

We would freeze the pizzas that were mistakes and write JESUS LOVES YOU on the pizza boxes. Then, we'd serve pizza along with the lunches to the people at the park. Even the owners and their children came down occasionally to help us feed. They were truly supportive.

I used to feed at 12:00 P.M. but because my co-workers (many of whom were high school students) wanted to join us, we changed the time to 2:15. It remains that time to this day.

By the time the students arrived at the restaurant it was already 1:45. Tack on a half hour for the ride and there you go. Week in and week out we would do this. My co-workers started bringing clothes, toiletries, and other things to hand out.

One of the owners, Michael, would occasionally give $50 and say, "This is for next week." How awesome is that?!

Unfortunately, the economy was so bad that the restaurant was forced to close. For the first time in my life I was about to go on unemployment. I kept thinking to myself, "What am I going to do about feeding the homeless?"

But as always, God showed up! People started supporting me, saying, "Michael, I've got next week's food."

Then another would say, "I have the week after."

It was truly amazing!

Michael told me one day that if I keep doing what I'm doing, others will step up and help me. He was right. I learned that people want to help doing things like this. They just have to know about it.

This took a lot of pressure off me. People did not step up all the time but when they did, the timing was always perfect.

I started going to flea markets after the restaurant closed to raise funds for the ministry having no idea that I would do this for many years.

The Sunday after the restaurant closed, I received a mind-blowing text at church from Michael of Pizza Fusion.

It read: *Mark (the other owner) and I want to have a super feeding for the homeless on Monday. Stop by the restaurant and let's cook some pizzas and go feed the homeless.*

Tears of joy flooded my eyes when I read that. They'd just lost everything, yet they still wanted to feed the homeless with whatever was still leftover.

We ended up making 50 large pizzas or so, then we drove to Lake Eola to love on the homeless in a delicious way. I will never forget that day. Nor will I forget the many other things Michael and Mark did for me and the ministry.

The best thing is, it was all done in Jesus' name!

A couple of years later, Michael's wife, Trina, asked me if her church worship band could come and play for our Monday night feeding. (I'll explain about the Monday night feedings later.)

I enthusiastically said yes. Needless to say, they were amazing. They provided all the instruments, including a drum set and band to JFJ (Jam for Jesus!).

They played for a good two hours. Many of the homeless danced to the music.

When it was over, Trina came up to me with tears in her eyes and gave me one of the best compliments I ever got. She said she and Michael lost everything when the restaurant closed, but they both concluded that the reason they opened the restaurant was to meet me.

I couldn't believe what my ears just heard.

I said, "Thank you Trina for the compliment. To God be the glory."

LOVE HIM BACK

Soon before the restaurant closed, the Lord put the words, "LOVE HIM BACK" on my heart. Up until that time, every lunch bag, pizza box, Christmas gift, etc., we handed out had the words, "JESUS LOVES YOU" written on it.

From that time on, we included the words, "LOVE HIM BACK" on the other side of the bags. It was then that "JESUS LOVES YOU, LOVE HIM BACK" became the name of the ministry.

In my prior life, I never told anyone Jesus loved them. Most of the words that came out of my mouth back then were truly meaningless, because they never glorified the One who saved me decades later.

But that was then. Now I will raise my hands and sing at the top of my lungs for Jesus, and only Jesus. Thanks to Him, I don't do cocaine today! Another Miracle! Can I get an Amen?

It was also during this time that we started our famous prayer circles, with our many volunteers after each feeding.

Sometimes we had a dozen or so people in the circle. Other times we had 30—sometimes even more than that. Despite how many were there, when we finished praying, I would always shout, "Jesus loves you…"

And everyone else in the circle would reply, "…Love Him back!

Those six beautiful words quickly became my motto.

To this day, I still don't know why God chose me to lead this ministry, but I'm so grateful He did!

RESTORING WHAT THE LOCUSTS HAVE EATEN

JOEL 2:25

Cocaine took everything from me! At the very top of the list was my wife and children. Everything else pales in comparison to that. The more I read God's Word and went to church, the more I realized that Satan wanted me back. He will never have me again, but he still tries all the time. Lust had been a big problem with me since I was delivered and now a Christian.

While working at Pizza Fusion, I was tempted by a handful of coworkers and customers. This normally played right into my hands, but not then (and not now).

I was a new creation trying to be obedient to the ways of God. but was still afraid the old me would come out; eventually it did. The sin was mounting big time with one of the handful. I had an affair with a woman for several months. Satan had me believe that what I was doing was fine. But it wasn't right, and I knew it.

There is nothing worse than knowing I was sinning and continuing to do it anyway. Things at this time were so crazy in my life. My mind was going a million miles an hour, as I said earlier, that's a bad place for me to be. I took my eye off the prize! This is what happens when I do! I even contemplated walking away from church and forgetting it all.

I was still a babe in Christ and wasn't deeply rooted yet. Psalms 1:1-3 NLT says, [1] "Oh the joys of those who do not follow the advice of the wicked, or stand around with sinners, or join in with mockers. [2] But they delight in the law of the Lord, meditating on it day and night. [3] They are like trees planted along the riverbank, bearing fruit each season. Their leaves never wither, and they prosper in all they do."

I wasn't even close to being this but now I strive for this daily. Once again, I take full responsibility for my sin. The praise report, however, is that through all the craziness, cocaine was never a consideration! This craziness is now a big part of my testimony. Thank you, Jesus!

I spoke to some of the elders at my church, confessed my sins, and repented. Truly repented! 1 Corinthians 7:9 says, "But if they cannot exercise self-control, they should marry. For it is better to marry than to burn with passion."

It had been 18 years since my divorce and I was finally ready for a new wife. There was no one in my life at that time who was to be Mrs. Higgins. I had Christian brothers praying for the right woman to come into my life. The one!!!

First John 5:14 says, "And this is the confidence that we have toward Him, that if we ask anything according to His will He hears us."

The key thing there is God's will. We can pray all we want but if it's not His will, it will NOT happen. In addition, it's also about His perfect timing.

In early December 2010, I started talking to a woman from Brazil who recently moved to the U.S. We had several conversations on the phone and agreed to meet for the first time at church that upcoming Sunday.

We didn't sit together but we met after the service. I was pleased with what I saw at first sight. Her English was broken but I understood some of what she said. Through our phone conversations, she knew about my ministry and where I wanted to take it.

Before we said goodbye after a 20-minute conversation, she pulled me over to a big window, opened her small Bible and started reading Matthew 25:31-46 to me in Portuguese!

Wow! That was an awesome moment for me. I didn't understand the words she spoke, but I felt them. I asked her if she would like to get together later that evening, and she said yes.

That was the beginning of our relationship. Before I knew it, she was my wife. Beforehand, I fasted for us three straight weeks. When I fast for the Lord, it's just that. I dedicate my fast to Jesus for everything He is doing in my life and for delivering me from cocaine, but when I need answered prayer or just advice I would fast for the answer.

It was said to me that when we fast for a specific prayer it sets off a spiritual atom bomb. I love the sound of that. I received a crystal-clear answer, I believed, saying she was to be my wife. On June 6th, 2011, she officially became Mrs. Higgins. Think about it, I'm from Philadelphia and she's from a small town called Catalao, Goias, Brazil and we met in a church in Orlando, Florida. God put us together for a reason! To glorify Him!

During that time, I had just started receiving unemployment checks for the first time in my life. Now with a wife to support, I had to put my complete trust in God. He has never let me down since I started walking with Him and He protected me when I was out in the wilderness!

God was starting to restore what the enemy had taken away. The pieces of the puzzle (God's plan) were starting to fall into place.

With my wife by my side, it was time to help expand God's Kingdom here on Earth with this feeding ministry...

TIME FOR OFFICERS, BOARD OF DIRECTORS, AND 501C3! ARE YOU KIDDING ME?

At this stage of the ministry, we only fed once a week at Lake Eola each Wednesday, but that was about to change. Many people kept telling me that God was going to greatly bless this ministry.

As it turned out, they were right. But the blessings we received up to that point had little to do with money. It amazes me even to this day (because of our availability) how we're able to do so much with so little to work with!

Anyway, God started sending people into my life to help take the ministry to the next level. Many later became officers and/or board of directors or officers. Imagine that, from snorting cocaine to attending board of directors' meetings. Isn't God amazing?

Our brother Nick did all the necessary work to get us incorporated. Three other men I knew from a Bible study gave checks totaling $850.00 to pay for the 501C3 application fee. We opened an account under *Jesus Loves You Love Him Back* and wrote the first check to the IRS.

While waiting for our 501C3 nonprofit status to arrive, an accountant helped us fill out the necessary paperwork to allow us to operate as a 501C3 nonprofit organization. Thank you, everyone, from the bottom of my heart for making this happen.

If anyone had told me I would have a board of directors, officers, and a 501C3 status for this ministry in the beginning, I would have had them committed!

OH, THOSE AMAZING MONDAY NIGHTS! I WAS HUNGRY AND YOU FED ME (MATTHEW 25:35)

Our former Vice President, Bhrett Black, said he wanted to talk to me about how we could expand the ministry. He told me about a church that allows organizations to feed the homeless in their parking lot without distractions. He said there was an opening on Monday evenings.

The only problem was that we didn't have the funds to do it. But after Bhrett kept assuring me that God would provide everything we would need to make this happen, I was eager to begin.

The following Monday was our "test drive," if you will. Using a small sound system, we read Matthew 25:31-46 to open the feeding (we read portions of the Bible each week to feed them spiritually before feeding them physically). When we served food to the homeless, we had Z88.3 playing in the background.

We expected to encounter a few problems that night, but when it was said and done, we fed more than 250 people. That was, by

81

far, our biggest feeding to date. With the assistance of 30-35 volunteers, we gave away clothing, toiletries, Bibles, feminine products, blankets, jackets, and backpacks.

I cannot put into words how wonderful I felt that night. I believe everyone who volunteered felt the very same way. When I got home, I couldn't wait to post the pictures from the feeding onto Facebook. My wife and I were exhausted but couldn't wait for next Monday to come so we could do it again.

We weren't the only ones. We received many phone calls the next day from volunteers saying how amazing it was and that they would be coming the following week with even more volunteers.

We've been serving every Monday night since. It quickly became the big event for us. Whereas Wednesday afternoon feedings at the lake were smaller in numbers and more intimate, this was like making it to the big leagues; at least for us!

As word kept spreading, praise and worship groups from local churches volunteered their time to perform for the homeless as we served them hot meals. We even had church groups come all the way from Alabama and Tennessee join us on Monday nights.

Pastor Kevin Kozial became one of our most dependable anchors almost from the beginning. Every other Monday night he would pack up his church bus with many people (most of them were homeless) and his equipment and drive 45 minutes to love on the homeless by performing for them. He even let them sing with him and play his instruments. He was a huge part of our Monday nights.

His heart for Jesus is truly inspiring. He understood what Monday night was all about. He loved the fact that we would never play secular music, never talk about politics, and never accept any of the praise. He knew Who received the glory.

Thank you, brother Kevin.

Every year at these Monday night feedings, we serve tens of thousands of meals, give out tons of clothing, assorted toiletries, and hundreds of Bibles, all in the mighty and precious name of Jesus!

In addition, we have thousands of volunteers who I believe get more out of it than the homeless people we feed. I know I do!

We also started feeding every other Saturday night at the same church parking lot location. This went on for a year or so, until we stopped to allow other groups to assume that slot, so they could also help bless the homeless.

Thank you, brother Bhrett, for your timely vision. We truly couldn't have started it without you! We have since moved on to another location but, make no mistake: Thanks to so many volunteers, Monday night had become our signature feeding.

TIME TO FEED THE GIRLS ON THE STREETS

Feeding the girls (prostitutes) on the Trail (Orange Blossom Trail) is always a special thing to me. The first night we did this we had more female volunteers than males for obvious reasons. These women have been abused by men in every way, shape, and form possible.

We made lunches and went to the Trail not knowing what to expect. In no time, we learned these ladies on the Trail were very grateful. Understandably, a handful of the them wanted nothing to do with us, but for the most part we were pleasantly surprised. We realized we had made more lunches than there were girls to feed, so we started fed the drug dealers, drug users, and anyone else in need of a meal.

I remember one day my wife handed a lunch to a drug dealer. Suddenly he started quoting scripture! I found this to be both ironic yet beautiful. I pray he is doing more than just quoting scripture now! It's sobering to see all the lost souls in need out there. They really are everywhere.

One night we were out on the Trail and we met a girl who was hungry and shoe-less. As she was eating her meal, Colleen, one of our volunteers, took off her shoes and gave them to her. This woman started crying and ran into Colleen's arms saying "thank you" many times.

There were two men observing who kept saying, "I can't believe what I just saw. Hallelujah!"

We prayed for them all and continued our "fishing expedition."

One night we bumped into one of the girls on the streets that we had fed before and she told us she had accepted Jesus as her personal Lord and Savior.

She offered to volunteer to feed on Monday nights and, lo and behold, she actually showed up! After several times of volunteering, she stated that she would like to be baptized. I had the honor of baptizing this woman.

Thank you, Jesus! I pray she is walking strong with the Lord today.

Anyway, getting back to Orange Blossom Trail, we would occasionally bring a youth group with us. Each time they joined us they would bring someone new to volunteer and something amazing always happened.

We literally pray for these women while standing in strip club parking lots or right there on the corner. Many of these women, due to their drug addiction, haven't eaten in days and often ask for a second lunch. You can tell who is really hungry by the way they eat. As soon as we bless the food and say amen, the bags get ripped open.

There have been some nights where we showed up to find a police sting operation going on, and the girls quickly scatter. When this happens, the Holy Spirit guides us to other places and Jesus always gets His glory!!!

FEET WASHING TIME! .... I WAS NAKED AND YOU CLOTHED ME (MATTHEW 25:36)

In the summer of 2013, my good friend and brother in Christ, Gilbert Montez, informed me that he was building a giant wooden shoe. Once finished, he placed it at a local YMCA for the sole purpose of collecting shoes for the homeless folks we feed each week.

I was overjoyed by the news and told him before giving the new homeless shoes to wear, I first wanted to wash their feet.

Gilbert loved the idea. When all was said and done, hundreds of pairs of shoes were collected for the homeless.

When we told our volunteers that we were going to have a feet-washing ceremony for the homeless, they were all in.

In addition to receiving shoes, hundreds of pairs of new socks, foot powder, lotion, and plenty of towels were donated to us as well.

The shoes were placed on tables in size order. We separated the men's from the women's shoes. We had the homeless form a line in which they could walk by the table, pick a pair of shoes and socks, and take a seat on the bench.

The volunteers then removed the dirty, dingy shoes and socks from the homeless folks gathered, threw them out, and washed their feet, all the while telling them Jesus loves them.

After the foot washing ceremony ended, the tables were cleaned and set up for dinner. When we were finished feeding, I washed the feet of our volunteers. It was a very emotional time for me.

I finished by washing my wife's feet. In return my wife and Bhrett washed my feet. Thank you, Jesus, for allowing us to feel so great inside! All we were doing was following Your lead.

Praise God, we washed hundreds of feet that day! It was an unbelievable feeling to say the least! Once again, we could have flown home that night without an airplane!

As we were setting up the tables and benches and lining up the homeless for their shoes, a very angry homeless woman was standing in line screaming and cursing at us.

When I finally heard her shouting, I asked her to stop. I told her we have children down here volunteering and they didn't deserve hearing that.

She screamed at me even louder to the extent that we had no choice but to escort her off the grounds. As she was leaving, she was cursing at me even louder. I think she invented curse words just for me!

About 10-15 minutes later, as we were washing feet, I felt a tap on my shoulder. I turned around and saw brother Gilbert standing there with this very same woman. She had tears in her eyes and asked me to forgive her.

I grabbed her hand, sat her down on a bench, and said, "I forgive you, and now let me wash your feet."

She said, "You can't wash my feet, I'm Jewish."

I answered, "So was Jesus, and He is the one who set the example."

She smiled and told me, "In that case, go ahead."

How great is God! That was the first of many feet washing events for us, and not just in Orlando.

Several weeks later, a local church was doing a fundraiser for *Jesus Loves You Love Him Back.*

When Bhrett and I walked into the church, we couldn't believe what we saw. The children painted our logo on poster boards and covered the walls of the church with it. We felt like rock stars.

They did an amazing job. The kids were pointing at us saying, "There they are! We always see you on Facebook!"

Wow! The senior Pastor told us he was a big fan of *Jesus Loves You Love Him Back* and that our work for the Lord was genuine.

He always watched what we did each week on Facebook. When he saw the photos of us washing the feet of the homeless, he said it touched him very deeply inside, to the extent that he washed the children's feet at Bible camp the following day!

How awesome is that?

When you do something in Jesus' name you never know how He will use it! After Jesus washed the feet of his disciples, he said, "[14] If I then, your Lord and Teacher, have washed your feet, you also ought to wash one another's feet. [15] For I have given you an example, that you also should do just as I have done to you. [16] Truly, truly, I say to you, a servant is not greater than his master, nor is a messenger greater than the one who sent him. [17] If you know these things, blessed are you if you do them. John 13:14-17.

Have you ever had the privilege of washing someone's feet in Jesus' name? If not, what are you waiting for? Try it, you'll like it!

PRISON MINISTRY TIME...I WAS IN PRISON AND YOU CAME TO ME (MATTHEW 25:36)

Let's go back in time. Do you remember when I applied for the Good News Prison Ministry and they never got back to me? I now believe that was part of God's plan and His timing. In short: He wanted me to start the feeding ministry before doing anything else for Him.

89

In 2010, a friend of mine invited me to attend a life group gathering. I met an awesome bunch of people that night! So much so that after it ended, I joined their life group.

That was where I first met Jeff Parker. Jeff came up to me after the meeting to introduce himself.

After telling him about my past and what Jesus was doing in my life, He, in return, gave me his mini testimony. We had so much in common. He then asked me if I knew about Celebrate Recovery.

I told him I had, but I didn't know much about it.

He informed me that Celebrate Recovery was having a Thanksgiving dinner party and asked if I would like to go with him. He said I would be an encouragement to the people there, so I gladly accepted the invitation.

I met many nice people there. In fact, three of the men I met are dear friends and, more importantly, my eternal brothers (Jeff Parker, Michael Ward, and Roger Throneburg), whom I will mention later.

At the end of the evening, they donated all the leftover food from the party to me for the next day's feeding—turkey, ham, stuffing, mashed potatoes, vegetables, pies, and all the fixings fit for a Thanksgiving meal for the homeless. They truly blessed the homeless on that Wednesday afternoon at the lake.

I've been going to Celebrate Recovery ever since. Celebrate Recovery is a ministry helping people with hurts, hang-ups, and habits. No matter what your kryptonite is—drugs, alcohol, lust, pornography, overeating, depression, whatever—they can help through prayer and fellowship.

Celebrate Recovery is a Christ-centered program. Mindful that only Jesus can truly break these chains plaguing humanity, Celebrate Recovery focuses on Jesus as the only true cure.

After being involved for two years, Jeff told me about the Celebrate Recovery Inside Prison Ministry. He asked if I would like to join him. I immediately said yes.

Praise God, I was quickly approved this time. This is when God wanted me to do prison ministry. His timing, not mine.

The first time I went to prison ministry I was hooked. I love these men and feel so privileged to visit them, especially knowing they are forgotten by so many.

Since I've been going there, some have received Christ as Lord and Savior. They may be behind bars, but their souls are freer than many souls living on the outside. I love this ministry!

One particular night after giving my testimony, a man came up to me and said, "Just yesterday the judge sentenced me to 690 years."

I gasped. I wasn't expecting to hear that.

He said he had no reason to live anymore but after hearing my testimony he felt a little more hopeful.

I suggested that he start reading the Bible, that all answers could be found in there. I didn't ask what he did to receive such a lengthy prison sentence, but whatever it was, he probably needed to be there.

I never saw him again after that night, and I don't remember his name, but if you would join me in praying for him—especially for his spiritual growth in prison—I would be grateful.

Another night after giving my testimony, a man came up to me and said, "I want to thank you for feeding me in Tampa."

I answered, "To God be the glory!"

He told me that when he saw me in Tampa, he had just gotten out of jail and hadn't eaten in two days. He really blew my mind.

Another night after I finished giving my testimony, a prisoner came up to me with tears in his eyes. He told me that I have a powerful testimony and that he was where I used to be.

I invited him to pray with me. I prayed, "Lord, I lift up this man who is where I used to be. Do for him what You did for me. Let him know You are real, Lord. Show him You are able. Deliver him from his kryptonite, so he can brag about what You did in his life for the rest of his days, in Jesus' name I pray, Amen."

We exchanged hugs and he walked away.

Suddenly, he turned back to me and said, "By the way, five months ago, you fed me in Sarasota before I got arrested. I was very hungry that day. Thank you."

Truth be told, I didn't want to go to prison ministry that night because I was exhausted. Look at what I would have missed!

Thank you, Jesus, for all these confirmations that make me want to do even more for Your glory and for the furthering of Your Kingdom here on Earth!

For four years, I went to prison ministry every Thursday night. I had to cut back to every other Thursday because of the growth of *Jesus Loves You Love Him Back*. But when I do go there, it's like we never miss a beat; we pick up right where we left off.

For a season, my wife even joined me in this ministry. What a blessing it was doing prison ministry with my wife!

Some of the most glorious moments took place when prisoners, after being released, came to one of our feedings for a meal and to thank us for visiting them in prison.

Every time I left prison, I always thanked God that I was visiting others behind bars instead of people visiting me. Thank You, Jesus!

TIME TO BAPTIZE IN JESUS' NAME

Before I begin with the baptismal testimonies I would like to share my own baptism story. This took place back in May of 2010, one year after I started doing the first feedings. What a memorable day it was for me! I was baptized at Cocoa Beach.

I still remember the song that was playing on the radio, when I turned on to A1A headed toward the beach—it was "In the Hands of God" by the Newsboys.

When we arrived at the beach, hundreds of people from my church were there. There were footballs and frisbees flying around everywhere. Many swam in the ocean before the baptisms took place. Everyone was enjoying themselves, my brother and I included.

Before I was baptized, I stared out at the ocean and couldn't wait to boldly declare in front of so many others that Jesus is my Lord and Savior and I am not ashamed!

The following year (2011), we brought 13 of our volunteers and homeless brothers and sisters to the beach, so they could be baptized with many from my church.

I asked the woman who owns the beachfront motel where our church baptizes (and is also a member of my life group), if we could feed the homeless after the baptisms. She gladly accommodated us. She even let them take showers before going back to Orlando.

How awesome is that?! This became an annual tradition with the ministry.

The second year (2012), we took 17 brothers and sisters to the beach to be baptized. The third year, 24 came with us.

Once a year we baptized at the beach. As our feeding ministry slowly expanded throughout Orlando, many of the homeless expressed an interest in wanting to be baptized. Instead of waiting a whole year for the next baptism with my church, we had to find another way to baptize them.

That's when Roger Throneburg stepped up to the plate. Roger is one of my very best friends. I take our friendship very seriously. Every time we get together, it's for Jesus' sake.

One day he told me, "Michael, I have a boat. We can take them out to the St. John's river and baptize them there."

He then told me he also wanted to be baptized. So that day my prison ministry partner, Jeff Parker and I, took Roger to be baptized, along with another dear brother in Christ, Kevin Atchoo, who said he wanted to be baptized as well.

WOW! What an amazing day it turned out to be!

Interestingly enough, many years later, Kevin Atchoo, who is a real estate agent, sold both the Parkers' and the Throneburg's houses.

That was the first boat baptism we did. Many more followed.

After we had baptized Roger and Kevin, Roger turned to me and said, "Start lining them up, Michael!" That's just what we did.

In the following months and years, we had the great privilege of baptizing many homeless people using Roger's boat which we named, "The Baptizer".

One of my best experiences was when we baptized three generations of a family at the same time. All were volunteers with us. At first, it was supposed to be the children only. We ended up baptizing their mother and grandmother as well.

We took them to a place on the river that has a little beach. Today we call that spot "Baptism Beach."

Roger Throneburg has since joined me and Jeff Parker at Celebrate Recovery Inside. Since then, we've baptized two ex-cons that we met in prison. We could have baptized them behind bars but, understandably, they wanted to be baptized upon their release.

As we head out to "Baptism Beach" Roger Throneburg always says his famous words: "This is the best part of church."

Roger probably wouldn't want me to include this in my book, but he pays for all the expenses for the baptisms out of his own pocket. He is such a blessing to the ministry. Thank you, brother!

PART FOUR:

TIME

TO

EXPAND

OUR

TERRITORY

BRAZIL

Matthew 28:19 says: "Go therefore and make disciples of all nations, baptizing them in the name of the Father and of the Son and of the Holy Spirit."

I was about to take my first trip to Brazil to meet my new family and feed the poor children while we were there. To raise funds for the mission part of our trip, Laiz and some of her Brazilian friends cooked Brazilian food. We sold tickets and had a fundraiser.

When all was said and done, we raised $800. In Brazil it was worth twice as much because of the 2-to-1 ratio over the Brazilian dollar at that time.

Friends of ours also donated toys and children's clothing, and 100 Bibles printed in Portuguese already waiting for us in Brazil.

After meeting my new family, we met Pastor Glauco from a local church in Catalao, Goias, Brazil.

We explained that we wanted to feed the homeless there but didn't know where to start. He asked why we chose this town and we told him it was Laiz's hometown.

Laiz took her time explaining the feeding ministry to Pastor Glauco. He and his wife seemed very serious. Since I didn't understand Portuguese, I felt a little awkward at first.

When she was finished, Pastor Glauco had a question for me. Laiz said, "Pastor wants to know if you are saved can you lose your salvation?"

Mindful of Romans 8:1, which declares, "Therefore there is now no condemnation for those who are in Christ Jesus," I said no. Anyone who thinks they can lose their salvation probably never had it to begin with. I said I take comfort in God's promise.

That put a big smile on the Pastor's face. He said he would be glad to help us. He even gave me the keys to the church. How cool is that? He said the kitchen was ours as often as we needed it.

What a great way to start my first international mission trip. It gave me the boost I needed.

We then met a woman named Gisselle who feeds the poor children in Brazil, in Jesus' name. She provided us with another boost in the arm.

Remember, we had no game plan, plus we had very limited resources. But after making ourselves available to serve others, God stepped in and opened doors for us. Just like that, we were serving in Brazil in Jesus' name. Isn't Jesus awesome?

This was my first Thanksgiving outside of America. I wanted to celebrate it by feeding the poor children.

My new family was "all in". They helped with everything from shopping for groceries, to separating the clothing, to writing *Jesus Loves You Love Him Back* in Portuguese in the Bibles, to cooking all the food and everything in between.

I couldn't believe how willing they all were to help. We went to Gisselle's house to prepare the food. We had toys for the children, from dolls to soccer balls. I started getting emotional when the children arrived. Laiz, speaking for me, shared my testimony and explained to them why we were there. They were so grateful.

Pastor Glauco gave a quick message and then blessed the food. Every child had more than enough food to eat. They all received toys and clothing. Most importantly, they received new Bibles.

Now they could follow along when Gisselle read the Word of God to them. We had roughly ten volunteers wearing *Jesus Loves You Love Him Back* T-shirts in Brazil who spoke no English but knew why they were there. Praise God!

After the first feeding, I was blessed to give my testimony at three churches, using my wife as a translator. If she wasn't there it wouldn't have been possible. She is from a small town and, as it was, I only met three people who spoke English there.

At one church, there were roughly 600 people in attendance. By far, it was the biggest church we'd visited to date. I glanced at Laiz and knew she was nervous. I told her to remain focused on why we were there and only repeat the words I spoke, to help calm her nerves. Gradually, she felt more comfortable and less nervous, and she started rambling on and on about my testimony.

As she spoke, the entire congregation was completely fixated on her. When their eyes suddenly volleyed back to me all at once, I thought to myself that perhaps she said something bad about my past and maybe they thought I was a mad man or something like that.

It was a bit uncomfortable at first, but I was trusting that she was testifying on my behalf in a truthful manor. When she was finished, everyone applauded so I assumed that through my testimony she gave God all the glory.

After the service, a man ran into my arms and was crying like a baby. Laiz wasn't there when it happened, so I had no idea what he was saying to me. When Laiz joined us, he explained to her how grateful he was to hear my testimony. He then told her he'd just been released from a drug rehab program.

He asked Laiz if we could go to the drug rehab center, so I could give my testimony to everyone there. I said absolutely. We went there two days later. What an experience it was for us!

Many there had the same problems I had battled much of my life, only in a different language and country. After sharing my testimony, I asked if they had Bibles. They said the rehab didn't have extra funds to purchase them.

We said we would try to get some Bibles for them. When we got back to the U.S., Laiz purchased Bibles and had them delivered to the drug rehab center. God bless you for that, honey!

We went to Pastor Glauco's church the following Sunday. After the service, we got busy preparing for round two of feeding the poor children. Again, I got emotional when the children arrived. This church had a soccer field on the grounds so as we prepared the food, the kids played soccer.

Before feeding anyone, Laiz once again gave my testimony and Pastor Glauco gave a short message and blessed the food. Just like last time, we handed out Bibles, clothing, toys, and food for the children. Only this time, they were even served ice cream.

Pastor Glauco truly loves Jesus and I know in my heart that I was meant to meet him. It truly was a 'God thing'. We are still great friends to this day.

Before we left to come home, someone told us about a family that happened to be in a very bad way. Sadly, the mother had died leaving the father to care for their 17 children. The poor man had to work two jobs to provide for his family, and even that wasn't enough. Their living conditions were nothing short of horrendous; the floor was made of dirt.

The walls consisted of thick plastic that was nailed to wooden beams. The children had bug bites all over their bodies. The only electricity they had access to was their neighbor's, who gave them permission to use it. Had it not been for that, they wouldn't be able to use the refrigerator in the kitchen, which stood next to the propane stovetop oven.

When I first met them, I was so saddened by their surroundings and living conditions, that we went to the supermarket and spent the rest of the ministry money, and even our own money, on food and other things they desperately needed. I wish I would have met them when we first arrived.

After leaving the store, we asked Pastor Glauco to join us, because we were leaving in a day or two, and we wanted him to be aware of their dire situation. He immediately got involved.

The next Sunday, he picked the children up in his church van and brought them to church service followed by Bible study. One Sunday, after picking up the children for church, he was able to clearly explain the Gospel to a woman who helped care for the kids.

Praise God, she received Christ as Lord and Savior! How awesome is that? Hallelujah!!!

It's quite remarkable what we were able to accomplish in just ten days in Brazil, with very little money and no predetermined game plan. How could I not praise God for opening so many doors for us?

I can't fully express to you how excited I get about sharing my testimony with others. Each trip to Brazil allows me to do just that.

To date, the biggest city we fed in was a place called Urberlandia. But regardless of city, the important thing is that I get to speak at different churches and share the love of Jesus with them. I also get to meet more people, which, as a true people person, is a good thing.

On two separate occasions, while walking around the lake, I was approached by pastors, and asked if I would be willing to speak at their churches. Even when my wife and I would go shopping, people recognized us. Some would point fingers at me and say they remember how my testimony had blessed them. Thank you, Jesus.

One thing I really enjoyed doing in my wife's home town was going to downtown Catalao for the sole purpose of handing out Bible tracks in Portuguese.

During Christmas week, Pastor Glauco and I did that on three separate occasions. I stood on one side of the street, he stood on the other side. I only know a few words in Portuguese. Three of those words are, "Jesus Te Ama," which means, "Jesus loves you."

If someone tried asking me something I told them I don't speak Portuguese and then said, "Jesus Te Ama."

Most replied saying, "Obrigado" (thank you). Seeing them reading the Bible tracts as they walked away was quite satisfying to me. I only hope that if they weren't already saved, the message in those small pamphlets opened their spiritual eyes and ears to the Gospel, and they repented of their sins and trusted in Jesus as Lord and Savior, thus sparing them an eternity in hell.

If you ever go to a country where you do not speak their language, I highly recommend bringing Gospel-centered Bible tracts along with you that are printed in their language. Then hand them out to everyone you meet and let the Word of God do the speaking for you. This is something God will definitely honor.

Lord willing, this outreach ministry in Brazil will continue to grow. Please keep us lifted-up in prayer for that.

TIME TO FEED ON THE
STREETS OF PHILADELPHIA

All I can say about feeding the peeps in Philadelphia is WOW!!!
To have the distinct privilege of feeding those who are still trapped
on the streets where most of my misery took place is difficult for
me to put into words!

For more than two decades, the only reason I was in this war zone of a neighborhood was to buy cocaine. In short, this neighborhood used to be my money pit.

Regardless of how I got the money—whether I worked for it or stole it—it always ended up in the hands of the drug dealers. They all knew my face. Some even knew my name.

Now that I was cocaine-free, I took my wife to Philadelphia to meet my family for the first time. There was no chance we weren't going to feed the homeless in my hometown! One morning we went to Walmart for food, then drove to my brother's house to prepare the lunches. My mother, brother, and two nieces were waiting for us to arrive, so they could help. Pretty awesome, huh?

After preparing the lunches, we picked up a man named Tony. I met Tony on Facebook a year earlier. As it turned out, he lived right across the creek behind my parents' old house. I praise God we didn't meet twenty years earlier. If so, it surely would have been a disaster waiting to happen. He has a similar background as me.

But God had other plans for us, by connecting us on Facebook, so we could serve together in Jesus' name.

What a blessing he is in my life to this very day. When we picked him up, it was as if we'd known each other all our lives. On one of our first phone conversations, Tony asked if I had a cousin named Andrew living in Feasterville (Pennsylvania).

I said I didn't think so.

He then said, "Good, now I don't have to apologize to you for stealing his car!"

I laughed and said, "Even if you did, I would forgive you. God bless you, brother."

I thought as we got closer to the war zone my stomach would be twisted in agony because of the many bad memories I'd created there, but that wasn't the case. I couldn't wait to get there so I could brag about Jesus and share with them what He did in my life.

As it turned out, we parked near the hospital I was rushed to twice, after having cocaine-induced seizures. Just looking at that building that day, knowing doctors there had saved my life twice—at least physically—filled my heart with gratitude.

I've taken my wife to some pretty scary neighborhoods in Orlando, but even during daytime, she never felt as frightened as she was in Philadelphia. But she also knew we were safe in the hands of God. I would have never brought her there at night.

We carried Walmart bags full of brown-bag lunches looking for mouths to feed. It didn't take long to find a bunch of homeless people. After asking if anyone was hungry and heard a very familiar response: "Yes, we're starving!"

After telling them we drove a thousand miles from Orlando, Florida to feed them and tell them Jesus loves them, they couldn't believe it. When I told them about the misery I endured in this neighborhood for more than two decades, many were inspired by it.

Some even said my testimony gave them hope. They saw a miracle standing right in front of them.

While preaching to them, I could easily see the pain in their eyes, as they saw Jesus in mine! It really hit me hard! My emotions got the best of me, knowing that used to be me.

For the first time in my life, I was in this war zone not for cocaine, but for Jesus! And this meant I didn't need to look over my shoulders in fear. The police were out monitoring everyone under the elevated train stations (El) but I had no reason to be concerned. I had nothing illegal on me!

Hallelujah! This trip only served to reinforce my testimony.

Every time we go back to Philly, we feed and plant Jesus seeds to all with a lot of love. Lord willing, this will continue long into the future, to include feeding the homeless in New Jersey, as we have already done on several occasions.

Lord willing…

TIME TO GO FISHING FOR MEN IN FLORIDA

When I first moved to Florida, I told my twin brother that I'd like to do more fishing. Little did I know I'd be fishing for men instead of fish! Aside from feeding in Orlando, it was placed on my heart to start reaching out to people in other cities in Florida...

As it turned out, Jacksonville and Tampa were the first two. We had no money to do this, but I knew God had placed it on my heart for a reason. The officers and board members knew we couldn't afford it, but they also saw what God was doing with this ministry and they agreed to keep trusting Him, despite our lack of finances.

We believed then, and still do to this day, that as long as we stay out of His way and always go out in Jesus' name, all will be well. So now it was time to back this plan with action!

105

JACKSONVILLE HERE WE COME

IN JESUS' NAME

It was on a Thursday in May of 2013 that we made 150 lunches and left for Jacksonville, Florida. Six of us made the trip. Brother Bhrett did the driving that day.

We set out at 2:00 P.M. and arrived at Jacksonville Beach a few hours later. We found a few homeless men who hadn't eaten all day. They were grateful for the food. I told them what Jesus was doing in my life and asked them where we could find more homeless people to feed. They directed us to a place two miles down the road.

When we arrived, we saw a bunch of homeless people there. They were everywhere, in fact!

When we got out of the car, we said to all who were listening, "We drove all the way from Orlando to tell you Jesus loves you." They were truly blown away and grateful. Think about it. This truly was radical love.

Everywhere we go outside of Orlando we now say this phrase. It is very powerful. They said they're occasionally fed by ministries and people in Jacksonville but never by a ministry from Orlando.

Once again, pretty cool, huh? After giving my mini testimony, we fed them and prayed for anyone in need of prayer.

A woman approached asking for prayer. She was crying like a baby. She told us she'd never been homeless before and she was frightened for her life! As we prayed, her sobs grew louder.

After we finished praying for her, I asked if she had a personal relationship with Jesus Christ. She said she didn't, but she wanted one. Wow! Praying with her to receive Christ as Lord and Savior was the highlight of the trip for me.

Everywhere we go to feed, we ask the Holy Spirit to prepare the hearts of all who would be rescued by God. I pray this was a Holy Spirit moment in her life.

Anyway, after receiving Christ as Lord and Savior, with my own two eyes, I could see her calming down. I pray her conversion was real and that I will see her again in Paradise.

When all was said and done, she went to a woman's shelter. After that, we drove to downtown Jacksonville. When we arrived, it was already 11:00 P.M. We saw many homeless people scattered about everywhere. We didn't leave until every lunch (Or should I say midnight snack?) was handed out in Jesus' name.

On our way back to Orlando, we were overflowing with joy and decided that we would go to Jacksonville once a month. We've never missed a month since. I find it amazing how many people are waiting for us when we arrive.

Many good things have happened while serving in Jacksonville. I can't help but get excited just thinking about what God will do to blow our minds next. Use us, Lord, as only You can…

TAMPA HERE WE COME IN JESUS' NAME

Two Thursdays later, we made 150 lunches and drove to Tampa, Florida. Four of us made that trip. We left at 1:00 P.M. Compared to Jacksonville, this trip was a hop, skip, and a jump.

As soon as we arrived, we pulled into a gas station on Martin Luther King Boulevard and Nebraska Avenue and fed 12 hungry men and women in Jesus' name.

Once again, we said, "We drove all the way from Orlando to tell you Jesus loves you." Like those we fed in Jacksonville, most were grateful.

We didn't find any large gatherings of homeless people in Tampa that day, only small clusters scattered here and there. We truly were fishing for men and God sure helped us find them! We prayed for the ones in need of prayer and told them we were going to try to be there every fourth Thursday of the month, Lord willing.

Now we have several 'watering holes' if you will, with five or six different spots to fish in Tampa...in addition to the stragglers we find. Just like in Jacksonville, we were filled with joy on our way back to Orlando and decided we would go to Tampa once a month as well.

We've met many people in Tampa and are excited to see who God puts in our pathway next. When You lead, we will follow, Lord!

DAYTONA BEACH HERE WE COME
IN JESUS' NAME

The following year, in May of 2014, while celebrating our one-year anniversary in Jacksonville, we decided to celebrate by expanding our feeding ministry to Daytona Beach, Florida.

We drove to Jacksonville first to fish for and feed the homeless, then it was off to Daytona Beach! By this time, we were known by many in Jacksonville and were warmly received by them.

When we told them that it was our one-year anniversary, they couldn't believe it. How time flies. We then told them we were headed to Daytona Beach next to feed the homeless there. They were happy to hear it.

We arrived in Daytona Beach around 5:00 P.M., and like the first time in Jacksonville, we ran into a few homeless men and told them we drove there from Orlando to tell them Jesus loves them.

It's amazing how such an easy phrase can comfort so many people. We told them it was our first time feeding in Daytona Beach and asked where we could find more homeless people to love on.

They led us to a park next to the city library. When we got there, the police were checking IDs to see if anyone had outstanding arrest warrants. When the police were finished, we fed them. They said this happened often. We asked if they knew any other spots we could go to feed, and they were happy to point us in the right direction.

Once again, when we arrived, the very same police officers were checking IDs again. We waited until they were finished before feeding the homeless there. Each location we went to that night had a solid police presence. This was truly an eye-opening experience for us.

While we do see police activity in other cities we feed in, it was nothing like this. Not even close. But even the police couldn't stop us from accomplishing our mission. On the way back to

Orlando, we knew we had to add Daytona Beach to our suddenly-growing list of places to feed each month.

So much good has come out of it so far. One of my greatest memories from Daytona Beach happened one Saturday when we showed up unannounced to find the homeless barbequing what they affectionately called "hobo stew", which consisted of hot dogs, baked beans, ground beef, and anything else they could add to it.

It was placed in a huge tin and smothered in barbecue sauce, then cooked on grills provided by the park.

After grilling the food that we brought for them, they asked us to try their concoction, which we did. After telling the man it tasted good, he told us the recipe always changed depending on what food and ingredients they had in their possession, and that it might be totally different next time. I'm glad I tried it. On a scale from one to ten, I gave it a five. Nuff said...

After eating, we played catch with them on the grass. As fun as the day had been up to that point, we had no idea that the main reason God sent us there in the first place hadn't even happened yet.

As we were packing the car for the ride back to Orlando, a woman I shared my testimony with earlier approached me saying she wanted to know Jesus like I knew Him.

After sharing the Gospel with her, she received Jesus Christ as Lord and Savior. She then asked to be baptized in the river situated next to the picnic area. What an honor it was for me! In fact, I'll go so far to say that it was one of the coolest moments of my life.

It was totally unexpected, which made it all the more rewarding.

Can I get an Amen?

Thank you, Jesus for using me.

ST. PETERSBURG HERE WE COME
IN JESUS' NAME

That same month, two weeks later to be precise, as we were celebrating our first anniversary feeding in Tampa, we decided to expand to St. Petersburg, which was 25 miles to the south.

After feeding in Tampa, we drove there and were quite surprised by the many homeless there. We were even more shocked to learn that (at that time) there were more homeless people (per capita) in St. Pete than anywhere else in Florida.

We parked at a downtown park to see bodies scattered all throughout the park. Seeing the bagged lunches, they picked themselves up off the grass and approached us.

It was unbelievable—almost like bodies rising from the grave. I will never forget the first time I saw that. When everyone was gathered, I said, "We drove all the way from Orlando just to tell you Jesus loves you." Like all other places we go to feed, most were touched by the gesture. Before feeding them, as always, I shared my testimony with them and read from God's Word.

In just minutes, all but four of the lunches were gone. Seeing four homeless men surrounded by police officers, I walked over to them and asked the police if I could feed them. They said yes but do it quickly because they were all going to jail.

I really appreciated that they let me feed them before they were handcuffed. Of course, I told them Jesus loves them. It was one of those moments in life where you just say, "Wow!"

As we were driving home from that trip, we knew St. Petersburg would be added to the list of monthly feedings.

How could we not, with so many there in need? What else could a servant of the Most High ask for?

MIAMI HERE WE COME IN JESUS' NAME

On January 31st, 2014, which just happens to be my oldest son's birthday, we expanded the feeding ministry to Miami. Of all the cities we travel to in Florida, Miami is the farthest to date.

My brother was with me on one of the trips to Miami and he put it in perspective. He said this trip is like driving from Philadelphia (the city of our birth) to Richmond, VA. and back to Philadelphia.

He was right. It's well over a 550-mile round trip. The traffic is horrific in both places. Anyway, that morning we made lunches and headed to Miami with no game plan except to fish for men. Boy did we find plenty of fishing spots!

The first stop we made was in downtown Miami. We got off at exit 2 on I-95, made a left on Miami Avenue, then another left on 6th street. We ran into a sea of homeless people; they were everywhere! It was truly a surreal moment for us.

The moment we got out of the car, they were lined up one after another waiting to be fed lunches. I shared my testimony with them before one of the board of directors and dear friend and brother in Christ, Richard, gave the message.

After that, we fed them. With the leftover lunches, we scouted out the area looking for more mouths to feed. It didn't take long for us to realize the great need in Miami. The question we kept asking ourselves was where is the church? This is something we say in every city in which we feed, but it's especially true in Miami!

Anyway, we drove up to an empty field and saw many homeless people there. We met a prostitute named Latoya. She was hungry and broken. After feeding her, brother Richard prayed for her. She started crying uncontrollably and received Jesus Christ as Lord and Savior. Her conversion truly felt genuine; I pray it was.

There was a crack house directly across the street from where we were feeding. It was evident that they weren't too thrilled to see us invading their home turf. There was this great presence of evil all around us. I can assure you the strength we displayed that day wasn't self-generated, it came from above. Otherwise we may have feared for our lives, especially since the police had warned us not to go there, that it was too dangerous a place.

Knowing our strength was Heaven-sent, instead of packing up and getting out of Dodge like the police said we would do if we were smart, we stood boldly for Christ saying, "Don't take their bag of drugs! Take our bag of food that was prepared in love instead."

Before leaving, I took the last three lunches we had and walked to a small patch of trees in the middle of a field where three men were sitting. One man had a needle in his arm full of heroin. Another one had a needle between his fingers. The third one was cooking up drugs on a spoon.

It caught me by surprise and I knew they were in no mood to hear me preach to them, so I left the lunches and said "eventually you'll be hungry. Jesus loves you."

One time as I was walking in the field, I noticed several people shooting up drugs. As I approached them, one man pulled a needle out of his arm and walked toward me demanding to know what I was doing in his neighborhood.

115

I told him I was there on behalf of my Lord and Savior Jesus Christ, and that we drove all the way from Orlando to tell HIM and everyone else that Jesus loves you.

He backed off when hearing this and even thanked me for the lunch. This happened in the Overland Park section of the city. Believe me when I say, it's not an area in Miami you ever see in postcards, especially in hell's bridge—a place we go to feed once a month! This place has had a profound impact on most who have fed there with us. Others seem frightened for their lives.

One time, a young girl at hell bridge who was high on drugs approached my twin brother wearing nothing but an oversized T-shirt. She asked if he would pray for her. After praying for her, my brother explained the Word of God so clearly to her that even someone high on drugs could easily understand it. She shed many tears and asked if we could give her a Bible to keep, which we did.

When we came back the following month, we learned she was hit by a car and died. We can only hope her conversion was genuine...

There was another man getting ready to shoot drugs into his arms. His arm was relaxed on a brick wall.

As I was handing out lunches and testifying this man stood straight up and said, "Out of respect for you and Jesus, I will not do this until you leave."

That was pretty cool. I pray God honors that. I pray that was his faith the size of a mustard seed and it will grow exponentially!!

I wish I could feed in Miami more often. It seems like no one cares for these people. I'm sure there are plenty of churches in the Miami area who feed the homeless, only we never see them when we are there. What we do see is great need, pain, hopelessness and despair. These things could be greatly alleviated if more of God's people would heed the Call and do their part to help.

While driving back from Miami the first time, Richard said something didn't feel right in Miami and that he wouldn't be coming back.

I said I completely understood how he felt but for me personally I saw an incredible opportunity for our feeding ministry, or as I sometimes say, there are many customers there. That evening Richard said he was awakened by the Holy Spirit and told to be a light in the darkness in Miami. He and his awesome son, Noah, make the journey with us on occasion!

One place in Miami you do see in postcards is Miami Beach. More than most places in the Sunshine State, this place represents the "haves" versus the "have nots" in such a way that it would make your head spin. When we go there to feed, our focus is solely on the "have nots".

One of the best "have not" stories I can share with you took place the night before I wrote this. Earlier that morning, my twin brother and I prepared lunches to feed the homeless in Orlando, Ft. Lauderdale and Miami. One of our volunteers picked up the lunches that were set aside for the homeless in Orlando, and my twin brother and I filled the minivan with the rest and left for South Florida.

After feeding many folks in Ft. Lauderdale and sharing the Word of God with them, we stopped at a local Walmart to purchase what we would need to feed the homeless the next day, then left for Miami.

Once we arrived at hell bridge, those who knew us were happy to see the boys from Orlando again, as they affectionately call us. It didn't take long before all the lunches were gone.

After feeding them, we checked into a hotel and treated ourselves to a Phillies-Marlins baseball game. When we got back to the hotel, it was just before midnight. It had been a long day and we were both exhausted.

Even so, my brother decided to go for a walk on the beach. I kept trying to talk him out of it, by saying it was late and he was tired and there were many bad elements out on the beach, but he was insistent on going. He never made it to the beach.

After spotting a small group of homeless people sitting on wooden benches under a pavilion on the boardwalk, he knew the reason he left the hotel was to meet them.

After explaining to them why we were in Miami, he called me confirming that we would be feeding them the next day.

I asked my brother to ask if they were hungry. They said yes. I told him to tell them I will make sandwiches and snacks for them and would be down in a few minutes with enough for everyone.

When my brother told one woman, who sat a distance away from the others, that food was on the way, she became teary-eyed. The expression of relief and gratitude on her face touched my twin brother deeply. To him, it was priceless.

When we handed her a brown paper bag a few moments later, I got to see it for myself. Personally, what I saw on her face only reinforced to me why God had called me to this ministry in the first place—to love on the least of these.

Though it was only eight people, they were so grateful, almost as grateful as we were to be able to feed them. Had my brother climbed into bed without venturing outside, God wouldn't have used us that night and they would have gone to sleep hungry.

Oh, to be chosen and used by God!

As you read this, how many homeless folks in your neighborhood will go to sleep hungry tonight because the "haves" in your city are too focused on their own lives to even think about the many "have nots".

Perhaps God is using this story to prompt you to go out and make a difference in the life of someone in your neighborhood.

If you are a true child of the Most High God, and you do it in the name of Jesus, your reward in Heaven will be great.

How awesome is that?

We now feed the homeless in Ft. Lauderdale each time we are in Miami. We even fed once in Key West, Florida, making it the furthest feeding point in Florida to date.

JESUS LOVES YOU LOVE HIM BACK IN MEXICO

My wife and I never had a honeymoon. But on our fifth wedding anniversary, we went to Cancun, Mexico to finally have one. Although it was only a four-night, five-day getaway, I told her I would like to feed the poor people in Mexico while we were there. She agreed so I got the ball rolling.

Having never been there before, I called my church and asked to speak to a Spanish pastor. After explaining my intent to her, she said she'd be more than happy to help us find a church in Cancun to show us where to go once we arrived, with a bi-lingual member who could translate my testimony to the congregation.

Within days, I was given an email address to a Pastor Daniel who has a church in Cancun. I emailed him explaining who I was and shared my intent to feed the poor there in Jesus' name.

Pastor Daniel replied later that day expressing his willingness to help us. And not only him, but his entire church. He also invited me to share my testimony with them.

I replied saying we would arrive the following week and would bring lunch bags, sandwich bags, and snacks with us. I asked if he would be kind enough to purchase enough bottled water, bread, lunch meat and cheese for us, we would pay him once we got there.

He agreed to do it. He excitedly told me his church had been looking for ways to reach out to the community and perhaps this would be their kick-off. Can I get an Amen?

When we got to our hotel in Cancun, Pastor Daniel and a few volunteers from his church met us there. He took us to his church where we were greeted by a dozen church members.

After exchanging pleasantries, two of them got busy writing *Jesus Loves You Love Him Back* in Spanish on the lunch bags we brought with us. Others cut rolls and loaded them with ham and cheese. Two children placed juices, cheese and crackers, and bags of muffins in the brown paper bags.

While observing it all, I thought to myself none of us knew each other five days ago; now were making lunches to feed to poor children in their country, in Jesus' name. It's as if we'd been doing it together for many years.

When we were finished, we prayed before heading out to the poorest section of Cancun. The 120 lunches we brought with us were gone in no time, given to many children and to poor families. The joy on their faces blessed us all immeasurably.

One thing I'll never forget from that trip was when we went door-to-door handing out food. We entered inside a small house that was filthy and full of mold. There was only one bed and many people living there. I gave a mini testimony to everyone. Pastor Daniel's wife, who is an English teacher, translated for me.

Thank you, Pastor. I truly couldn't have done it without you. It's amazing how something can be put together in such a short time when God is in control...

After the feeding, I was honored to give my testimony through Pastor Daniel's wife, Rakuel back at his church.

Lying in bed that night, I felt so blessed to have spent our first full day in Mexico serving others in Jesus' name.

Upon returning from Mexico, one of our Wednesday volunteers, a woman named Eunice, saw our pictures on Facebook. She was going to Mexico in a couple of weeks to visit her mother and expressed an interest in volunteering her time with Pastor Dan's church, to re-water the seeds we'd planted, so to speak.

Before leaving for Mexico, Eunice spoke to Pastor Dan on the phone. He confided in her that the church needed a new projection screen. Along with another volunteer, a woman named Celimar, Eunice shared this at their women's prayer group.

Everyone was eager to help make it happen. One woman even made jewelry to sell to help the cause.

Upon arriving in Mexico, Eunice traveled two hours to Pastor Dan's church to help them feed the poor and give him the money they'd raised for a new projection screen. How cool is that?

I always love hearing about these "under the radar" moments that the world never gets to hear about, yet they're all recorded in Heaven by God Almighty Himself. Wow, just wow!

JESUS LOVES YOU LOVE HIM BACK
IN NEW ORLEANS

In Spring, 2017, Gilbert Montez—one of the ministry's most faithful servants who built the wooden shoebox, so we could collect shoes for the homeless—asked if I would like to go on a mission trip with him to Baton Rouge, Louisiana.

Technically it was Denham Springs. Organized through Operation Blessing, which was founded by Pat Robertson, our job was to gut homes that had been flooded before they could be repaired.

I enthusiastically agreed to go with him.

When we arrived there, we met many volunteers from all over the country. It was awesome to see. We worked our tails off, but it was very rewarding. They fed us breakfast and dinner daily, and we slept on cots each night in a local church in the men's section.

Among the awesome volunteers we met was a group of Mennonites from Texas. Every morning when we woke and every evening before going to sleep, they serenaded us with old-time gospel music. And could they sing! It was so beautiful.

They were a joyful bunch of men who always had smiles on their faces, even when working. Our bodies ached each night, but it was a good kind of pain.

The fact that Gilbert did this kind of work for a living meant that he was in his element. As for me, I did the best I could.

On our last day there, we decided to drive to New Orleans to feed the homeless there, before going back to Florida. When we shared this with the other volunteers, they helped us make the lunches. Needless to say, we were grateful.

After breakfast that day, along with 20 or so volunteers, we made 150 bagged lunches. Before leaving for New Orleans, we prayed together and said our goodbyes.

As much as I loved gutting homes and cleaning up messes, feeding the homeless put me more in my element, so to speak.

The closer we got to New Orleans, the more excited we were, knowing we were going fishing for men in the *Big Easy*.

When we first arrived, we barely saw any homeless people. Finally, when we got to Bourbon Street, we fed approximately 15 of them. All around Bourbon Street, we literally felt evil dripping off the buildings. That place needs more people to be lights for Jesus!

When we left Bourbon Street, in search of a gas station, so we could fuel up. Finding one five minutes away, we had to make a U-turn to get to it. It was there that I saw a hundred or so homeless men and women on the other side of the street.

My eyes lit up, "Gilbert, look at all the homeless people across the street!"

He looked and smiled and we both said, "Thank you, Jesus."

After filling the tank with gas, we crossed the street carrying every bagged lunch we had. Like most other places, they were completely blown away after hearing we drove all the way from Orlando, Florida just to feed them and tell them Jesus loves them.

After showering the homeless with radical love, Gilbert and I treated ourselves to a Cajun dinner. Man, what a wonderful feeling we both had driving back to Florida!

I pray that God will open the door for us to feed in New Orleans again someday, in His mighty name. Lord willing...

JESUS LOVES YOU LOVE HIM BACK
IN CHICAGO

I have always wanted to go on a mission trip somewhere in the United States with just the boys. In March of 2017, my twin brother told me that Chicago was on his heart. A day later it was also on mine.

At that time, the murder and crime rate in Chicago was off the charts. Sadly, it hasn't improved. If anything, it's only gotten worse.

One of the ways we raise money for the ministry is by having fundraisers at local supermarkets in Central Florida. Topping the list is Publix supermarket. They have been so good to us. I honestly don't know where we would be without their help.

The money we raise there comes by way of donations from shoppers at their stores, which is mostly used to feed the homeless in the Sunshine State. But the coin donations we receive, which is ample at times, is earmarked for mission trips to cities outside of Florida, where we hadn't yet fed the homeless.

Though the change we collected leading up to that trip wasn't enough to fund the entire trip, it paid for a good chunk of it. A total of seven volunteers made the trip to Chicago, eight including my good friend, Cory, who lived in the suburbs of Chicago. Another good friend and brother in Christ, Michael Ward, drove his 18-wheeler from Georgia to Illinois to join us.

My two biological brothers, Kevin and Brian, flew in from Philly, as did a good family friend of many years, Charles Culmer. Yes, the one who often stopped by whatever restaurant I worked at during my drug addiction days to pray for me. Now he was amazed seeing what God was doing in my life.

As for me, my twin brother, and volunteer coordinator, Joshua Mendez, we rented a minivan, packed it with the things we would need for the trip, and drove from Orlando to the Windy City.

We left Orlando on May 1. Initially, we planned to drive straight on through to Chicago, but as the day progressed we grew tired and decided to spend the night in Frankfurt, Indiana.

When we woke the next morning, while having breakfast in the hotel lobby, my brother had suggested that we make the lunches before checking out. This way, when we arrived in Chicago we could hit the ground running, so to speak.

I went to the front desk and asked if we could make lunches in the breakfast area. Not only did the woman, who just happened to own the establishment, say yes to my request, her daughter and parents helped us make 225 lunches for the homeless in Jesus' name.

After the lunches were made, I asked if I could pray for them. They said yes. What made it even more remarkable was that they were Hindus! We held hands and prayed, asking the Holy Spirit to draw their hearts to Jesus, and also that God would richly bless them for their service to our ministry.

When I finished praying, the mother and daughter both had tears in their eyes. How awesome is that? I pray that God rescues them from their false religion and gives them eternal life through Christ Jesus!

After checking into the hotel in Chicago, near O'Hare International Airport, we drove downtown with Cory—who'd met us at the hotel—looking for homeless people to feed. It was both gratifying and satisfying to be fishing for men in the Windy City.

It didn't take long for all of the 225 lunches we prepared in Frankfurt, Indiana to be handed out in Jesus' name. It was a great way to kick off the mission trip. I'll never forget a man I met named Brian. He lived in a tent that was situated under a small overpass bridge near Lakeshore Drive. It was a stone's throw away from Lake Michigan. The strong steady winds blowing off the lake that day ripped through us like a hot knife in butter.

I knocked on Brian's tent and handed him a bagged lunch. As I shared my testimony with Brian, he started to cry, saying he was where I used to be.

After praying with him, I told him we would be in Chicago the next five days and that we would feed every day we were there. He was very grateful.

The next morning after having breakfast in the hotel lobby it was off to Walmart again to purchase everything we would need to feed that day.

As always, we told everyone we fed that we drove all the way from Orlando to tell them Jesus loves them, and they were blown away. On day two, we got to say that in addition to us driving all the way from Orlando, Kevin, Brian, and Charles flew in from Philadelphia, and Michael drove all the way from Georgia.

We repeated that gesture every day we were there—feeding hundreds of homeless and truly loving on them.

Having my two brothers and Charles fly in from Philadelphia to feed the homeless with us in Chicago, in Jesus' name, was beyond description. All three were instrumental in making that mission a success.

Growing up as Phillies fans, we were treated to a Phillies-Cubs game at Wrigley Field. To be able to go there with our brothers from Philly was a bucket list thing. It was bitter cold that day and I told my brothers because it's so cold the game would probably go extra innings. Sure enough, it did.

By the time the game had reached the thirteenth inning, even though we are huge Phillies fans (not counting Michael Ward and

Cory Lewis), it was so cold that we joined the Cubs fans shouting, "Let's go Cubs! End this game!" I know it was lame of us to jump off the Phillies' bandwagon so quickly, but it was so cold that day, you'd think we were at a Bears-Eagles game in mid-December rather than a Cubs-Phillies game in May.

At any rate, the Wrigley Field experience was everything I could have ever hoped it would be. The only thing that would have made it better was if my brother Jim and my late father were with us.

After the game, we went out feeding again. We met this Vietnamese couple who had been married for 30 years and had a feeding ministry in the Windy City.

They took us to several underground places in downtown Chicago where the homeless slept. Despite that many rats could be seen in many places, the homeless slept there because it was better than freezing to death out on the streets.

One of them, after being handed a bagged lunch, told us if they didn't eat their lunches right away, the rats might help themselves to it.

After feeding at a few other downtown locations, this wonderful Godly couple treated us to an awesome Vietnamese meal. How cool is that? They said next time we visit Chicago they'll show us even more places where the homeless stay. Don't tell me that was not God!

On a personal note, Brother Joshua really shined in Chicago. Remember, it was just two years ago that he was homeless himself, and in a very bad way. Now he was wearing new clothes, he smelled good, and had a new haircut and he really looked like he belonged at the hotel instead of like the old days when he was always being asked to leave the premises.

Every time the staff at the front desk saw him they would say "Hello Mr. Joshua!" His face lit up each time, and he broke into the warmest of smiles. He felt like he was the owner of the hotel!

Early each morning, he would join the team for breakfast in the hotel lobby restaurant, before going to Walmart for the necessary things needed to feed for that day.

127

Before leaving the hotel to feed the homeless in downtown Chicago, Joshua would ride the elevator car down to the lobby floor with a luggage cart full of bagged lunches. After putting them in the van, he would repeat the process until all lunches were in the car.

Joshua truly inspired not only our team of volunteers but everyone who worked at the hotel. I'm so proud of you, Joshua!

Chicago was a complete success in Jesus' name. It was great to say those two awesome words with the team and those two words were Mission Accomplished—at least for that trip!

JESUS LOVES YOU LOVE HIM BACK
IN LAS VEGAS AND LOS ANGELES

In June of 2017, my wife and I took a mission trip to Las Vegas and Los Angeles. What an unbelievable experience we had! When we landed in Las Vegas the temperature was 117 degrees.

If you've never experienced that kind of heat before, try to imagine a blow dryer hovering above your city or town, turned on full blast, blowing hot air in your face all day. Within hours, my throat was sore. We chose Las Vegas because of its name—Sin City. We knew there would be many there to love on.

After checking into our hotel, we went to Walmart for the things we needed, made 150 lunches, and went fishing for the homeless in Sin City. It was my first time in that city in more than 30 years. It's not the same town in any way, shape, or form. It grew up in a big way. Praise God, so did I.

With extreme heat warnings issued, we drove all throughout the city, finding and feeding the homeless. The excessive heat warnings remained in effect the six days we were there. It was stifling hot!

I couldn't understand why the homeless had to fend for themselves in those unbearable temperatures. With schools closed for summer vacation, you would think they would've opened a gymnasium or two to help keep them cool and hydrated.

Aside from the two of us, the only other people we saw helping the homeless was a couple handing out cold water to them. I'm sure many others feed the homeless in Las Vegas, including churches, we just didn't see them. The homeless were so grateful.

Once again, we got to say, "We flew all the way from Orlando, Florida to tell you Jesus loves you!" I know I sound like a broken record, but it truly is radical love.

When we got back to the hotel, we were exhausted! But nothing would stop us or even slow us down to accomplishing our mission, including the stifling heat.

129

On day two, we found a place where roughly a hundred homeless people were staying. It was definitely "the hood" of Las Vegas. When we got out of the car with lunches in hand, the Las Vegas police were there. We asked if we could feed the homeless there and they said yes. They even thanked us for doing it.

After hearing where we were from, they told those we were there to feed to treat us with respect, which they did. Never once did my wife or I feel like we were in danger. Then again, we knew we were being supernaturally protected no matter what.

It didn't take long to hand out all the lunches. Now that we knew where we would be feeding the next three days, it gave us more time to spend with them and read God's Word to them. Even in the blazing heat, they were really receptive to it. Many seemed hungry for God's Word.

Thank you, Lord, for making that happen.

One man who was eating his lunch asked me where we made these lunches. We told him we woke early in the morning to purchase the things needed to ensure that their lunch was freshly prepared and then we went back to the hotel to prepare them.

He had a tear in his eye and said we were probably the only two people in all of Las Vegas making lunches in a hotel room for the homeless. He kept thanking us and we kept giving God the glory.

It made us feel good inside but also sad to think that what he said was most likely true.

The last day in Vegas was a bit strange—but in a good way. Saying our goodbyes to our new friends (hopefully many were new brothers and sisters in Christ) was like saying goodbye to people we'd known all our lives. They were so grateful yet sad that we were leaving. Two guys, both named Michael (go figure), came up to me at two different parks and hugged me and asked if I could pray for them again. Both men had tears in their eyes after the prayer and I truly pray that God answers them.

The next day, we woke at 5:00 a.m., made 150 lunches and left for L.A. Since my exodus from California in the 80s, I was in the Golden State with my brother only one time, on a business trip in the 90s. Now drug free, I was excited to be back in the City of Angels.

It took four hours to get there. The closer we got to L.A., the more excited I got. Memories flooded my mind of days living in North Hollywood—both good and bad. The good news was that the bad memories were just that, memories! But more importantly, I was forgiven those bad memories! Thank you, Jesus.

Thirty years ago, I left there a complete mess. Now I was returning a new creation with a message of hope to share with all who would listen! We headed to downtown L.A., specifically to a place called skid row. When I lived in L.A., I'd never heard of that place.

When we arrived, it looked as if we'd driven into a war zone! I hadn't felt this overwhelmed since my first trip to downtown Miami. I had always called Miami "Baby L.A.", but downtown Miami dwarfs in comparison to downtown L.A. This is even true regarding the homeless.

Everywhere we looked we saw a sea of downtrodden homeless people! We drove around not knowing where to park, let alone where to begin. All we knew was that we didn't have enough lunches for everyone. Not even close! In your mind, try picturing eight city blocks going in every direction full of tents, makeshift tents, cardboard boxes, and hundreds of lost and hurting people, and you will have a pretty good idea of what we encountered that day.

We finally parked the car. As soon as they saw us taking lunches out of the car, they swarmed around us in large numbers. I didn't get to give my full testimony, but I made sure they knew we were from Orlando and that we were there in Jesus' name.

I told them what Jesus was doing in my life and that He was able to do the same for them. We blessed the food and then it was a free for all!

I handed out lunches fast and furious and so was Laiz. Just like that the lunches were gone, and I realized I couldn't see my wife. I walked to the corner and looked to the left and saw her handing out her last lunch about 50 feet away.

I ran up to her and said, "You did a great job, but don't ever leave my side again in a situation like this!"

We never felt like we were in danger, because we know that whatever happens we're protected but we still need to be aware of our surroundings. She didn't do anything wrong, it's just the feeding of the homeless led her up the street. I was very proud of her—she had no fear.

Many were blown away when they learned we'd come all the way from Orlando to feed them. Some were disappointed when we ran out of lunches but most understood and were grateful that we could feed as many as we did. How cool is that?

When we left L.A., I felt sad in my spirit for the many who were lost and hurting. Even as I write this, I still can't remove them from my head or heart. If it's God's will, we will go back to L.A. and Las Vegas with even more volunteers and make sure we have enough food, clothing, toiletries, and Bibles to hand out.

JESUS LOVES YOU LOVE HIM BACK
IN NASHVILLE, TENNESSEE

Nashville was a spur of the moment mission trip for the most part. Brother Gilbert Montez and I were once again going somewhere to preach the Gospel, just like we did in New Orleans.

We stayed in the home of a lovely family, who started out as Gilbert's friends but when we left, they were mine as well. We landed early in the morning in Nashville and hit the ground running.

We went to Sam's Club to buy the food for the lunches and realized we were a good 20 miles away from where we were staying and 20 miles away from where we were going to feed. Brother Gilbert asked for the manager of the store and told him who we were and what we were doing.

Gilbert explained the geographical situation and asked if we could make the lunches there at Sam's Club to save time.

The manager agreed to let us do it. In fact, he was quite enthusiastic about it, and allowed us to make the lunches in the 'food court' area of the store. How awesome is that?!

Many employees and shoppers asked what we were doing. Upon hearing that we'd just flew in from Orlando to feed the homeless in Nashville for the next five days, many were amazed.

We also made sure to brag on the manager for being so kind to let us prepare the lunches in his store. Many thanked us for caring enough to feed people in their city. Some were moved to tears...

We quickly ran out of lunches. We told those we fed that we would be in Nashville for five days and, Lord willing, we looked forward to serving them each day and spending time with them.

They were truly grateful.

One man came up to me and thanked me for the lunch. He then thanked me for feeding him many times when he was living in Jacksonville, Florida. Wow! I love hearing stories like that.

The next day, another man came up to me and said the same exact thing and they didn't even know each other.

On Saturday, we partnered with a ministry called the 615, which is Nashville's area code. Their weekly feedings are so much bigger than ours. Even so, we do the same thing in that we both give God all the praise, honor and glory.

If you're ever in the Nashville area and want to serve the least of these, I highly recommend searching for the 615 group.

JESUS LOVES YOU LOVE HIM BACK
IN THE PHILIPPINES

Aside from my twin brother's busy career as a Christian author, he has a ministry in the Philippines, which began in 2006.

Besides preaching the Word of God to many over there, he also feeds the poor and homeless. The first feeding my brother sponsored in the Philippines was back in 2011, after a typhoon ripped through the southern part of the country—in Mindanao—

causing widespread flooding throughout the region. Many lives were lost, and many homes were destroyed.

At that time, my brother had just finished writing a book that took place in the Philippines. He decided to send all proceeds from book sales directly to flood victims, asking friends to purchase books here in the U.S. He even spoke in Filipino churches in America seeking donations to send to their home country.

Many rose to the occasion and gave generously. The money was then wired to trusted individuals in the Philippines, who did the rest, providing hot meals for those who'd lost everything. Some of the kind-hearted volunteers were flood victims themselves.

My brother's focus now is on feeding the street children over there. Much like in Brazil, and unlike here in America, there aren't many options for homeless children to exercise over there.

It has been an honor and blessing for *Jesus Loves You Love Him Back* to co-sponsor some of those feedings. The first one was in 2016. We have co-sponsored a few more since.

Some of the volunteers over there asked, and were given permission, to download the *Jesus Loves You Love Him Back* logo so they could make T-shirts to wear when feeding the least of these.

How awesome is that?

We recently shipped a package loaded with *Jesus Loves You Love Him Back* T-shirts and wristbands, and clothing for the children over there. To date, the Philippines is the forth country where volunteers feed the homeless wearing our *Jesus Loves You Love Him Back* T-shirts.

Lord willing, we will continue sponsoring feedings there in the coming months and years, and send even more shipments to them...

LOVE IS CONTAGIOUS

God never ceases to blow my mind with the people He has sent my way. Thousands of volunteers have joined us in the ten years we've been feeding the homeless, ranging in age from 1 to 90!

Some have since started spin off feedings of their own. One of the first was started by a group of UCF students (University of Central Florida). Roughly 30 to 40 volunteered their time with us feeding the homeless. This went on for 4 months or so.

One Monday night before the feeding, the group leader told me this would be their last feeding with us. When I asked why, he told me they would be starting their own feeding program beginning the following Sunday! I was amazed by what my ears had heard!

I thanked them for their service and told them how honored I was to have them volunteer their time with us. As far as I know, they're still feeding to this day. Thank you, Jesus!

Another man, after feeding with us for two years, eventually branched out and started feeding at another location every other week. And two of the churches and life groups who fed with us on occasion, have since branched out and are now feeding in two local cities in Florida.

What can I say? God is on the move!

In January 2015, I went to Philadelphia to visit my family with my twin brother. While visiting a friend (who knows all about my past), he asked if I would like to give my testimony at his church.

Of course, I said I would love to! After clearing it with his pastor, I met him the Friday evening at a Bible study. As we talked, the pastor said he would love for me to give my testimony.

He then said, "I understand you will feed the homeless while you're here."

I told him I wanted to feed on Monday because it was Martin Luther King Day. He said we could make the lunches at our church kitchen. He then encouraged me to invite the congregation to join me, insisting that some would surely be interested in helping.

On the day I gave my testimony, approximately 40-50 people were there to listen. When I was finished, I told the congregation I would be feeding the homeless the next day, and if anyone wanted to join me, we'd meet at the church at 10:00 A.M.

Since it was bitterly cold outside, I asked them to bring any extra jackets, blankets, socks and sweaters they'd like to donate to the cause. I also asked them to bring any extra food from home that they weren't going to eat, so long as the expiration date hadn't already passed. We already had plenty of food, but I figured why not fill the bags to the brim?

The next day, my twin brother and I arrived at the church, to find 50 people or so waiting for us in the basement kitchen, ready to serve in Jesus' name. Hallelujah! Even as I write this, tears of joy fill my eyes. They even brought jackets, blankets, socks, sweaters, toiletries, food, and much more.

We cranked up K-LOVE radio and got busy making lunches. Once we were finished, we formed a prayer circle and Brother Jason read Matthew 25:31-46 aloud to everyone.

I then spoke for a while, and was quite emotional, before Pastor prayed us out before going out in the trenches. We ended up feeding and clothing many who were cold and hungry that day in Jesus' name. I feel certain that we made our King smile.

Afterward the pastor called me an inspiration, saying he would never forget the impact the feeding had on him. Even better, he told me his church would take the torch, so to speak, and keep feeding the homeless from that location on a monthly basis! Wow!

My twin brother and I went back to Philadelphia later that year, to spend Christmas with our family, and attend the Christmas Eve service at this church. Not only were they still feeding on a monthly basis, the pastor told me the church would be feeding the homeless the following day, Christmas Day to be precise!

Like I said—love is contagious!!!

In my home state of Florida, I met a man named Andrew Gibson during a fundraiser at a local supermarket. He told me he was volunteering with another group, but that it really wasn't for him.

He then asked about how our ministry works. I told him we feed the homeless, plain and simple! Whether hot meals or bagged lunches, whether they come to us or we go to them, the important thing is that we do it all in Jesus' mighty name.

Ever since that time, Andrew's been serving with us in some capacity. In addition to feeding on Monday nights, and occasionally traveling the state of Florida with us, he also goes out on his own on Saturdays and Sundays feeding in Jesus' name.

Andrew has an infectious smile that always inspires me. Even better than that, he doesn't tell me what he will do, he just does it. He occasionally sends pictures—via text message—as he feeds the homeless. It never ceases to put a smile on my face.

God bless you, Andrew. Keep on Jamming for Jesus!

My good friend and brother in Christ, Jeff Bradshaw, who is a faithful supporter, board member and volunteer—he even preaches the Word on occasion at our Monday night feedings in downtown Orlando—went on vacation in Mexico with his wife, Debbie.

One Easter Sunday I glanced at my Facebook account and, lo and behold, I saw pictures of Jeff and Debbie making lunches and writing *Jesus Loves You Love Him Back* on the containers.

They fed the poor and homeless in Mexico on Easter Sunday—while on vacation! How awesome is that! Love truly is contagious.

In closing this section, these are just a handful of examples of how God is using this wonderful feeding ministry for His glory and for the furthering of His Kingdom here on Earth.

To date, more than 250,000 meals have been served in the mighty name of Jesus...and counting.

Not only that, professors from two local universities in Central Florida have recently taught about my feeding ministry. Like I said at the outset, I never went to college, yet universities are now teaching about *Jesus Loves You Love Him Back* feeding ministry!

Imagine that...And to think it all started 10 years ago at Lake Eola, in downtown Orlando, when I fed 25 lunches to homeless folks for the very first time with this feeding ministry. Little did I know it would lead to all this. To put it into perspective, those 25 lunches amounted to only .0001% of what we've served since then.

Wow, just wow! Lord willing, this is just the beginning of God opening even more doors for us to serve in His name, as time marches on. Thy will be done, Lord, Thy will be done...

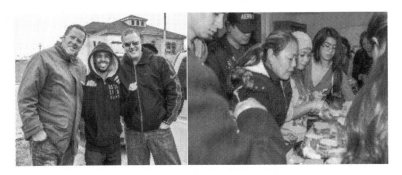

PART FIVE:

THINGS

I'VE

LEARNED

ALONG

THE

WAY

IT'S NOT ALL A BED OF ROSES

One thing I've learned along the way is if you serve long enough in any field of service in which our Lord may call you—not only feeding the homeless—you are bound to encounter your fair share of ungrateful individuals along the way.

These people will do their best to make you feel as if your efforts aren't necessary, that you aren't making a real difference. They will mock and criticize you, judge you and constantly complain. Some can be so convincing at times that you may feel like giving up.

Don't get me wrong: most people are grateful for the food we give them. Even so, when we encounter the ungrateful ones, it still hurts. Whenever this happens, I always try to remind myself that my walk with God is so much more than mere feelings; it's the understanding that something far greater awaits me on the other side.

The good news is, if you are a true Christ follower, you can claim this same eternal promise for yourself! But for now, as we continue on our journey on this fallen planet, we should expect these types of people to visit our lives along the way.

Next time this happens to you, direct your hurt feelings to the words the Disciple Peter wrote in the book bearing his name: 1 Peter 4:14 declares, "If you are insulted for the name of Christ, you are blessed, because the Spirit of glory and of God rests upon you."

In verse 15, Peter then warns, "But let none of you suffer as a murderer or a thief or an evildoer or as a meddler."

What Peter is saying here is if you suffer or are being persecuted for bad things you have done, that can never be considered as suffering for the Kingdom. Common sense should dictate that much.

After giving us that stern warning, Peter once again encourages all believers in verse 16 by exclaiming, "Yet if anyone suffers as a Christian, let him not be ashamed, but let him glorify God in that name."

He then ends chapter four with these comforting words found in verse 19: "Therefore let those who suffer according to God's will entrust their souls to a faithful Creator while doing good."

Comforting words indeed…

The point to consider is that Satan wants you to feel discouraged in your service to our Lord. Remember the ultimate enemy of God is also humanity's ultimate deceiver! That said, it is the devil's hope that you will one day give up and abandon your service to God!

As Christians, we should expect to meet mockers and deceivers at every turn. Jesus Himself warned that the world hated and persecuted Him. All who follow Him should expect the same.

With that in mind, I encourage us all to wear the criticisms we suffer for the Cause as badges of honor that will one day be exchanged for eternal rewards. Can I get an Amen?

If there's one example I can give to put things into perspective, it would be when Jesus cleansed ten lepers. Luke 17:11-19 says, [11]On the way to Jerusalem, he was passing along between Samaria and Galilee. [12]And as he entered a village, he was met by ten lepers, who stood at a distance [13] and lifted up their voices, saying, "Jesus, Master, have mercy on us."

[14] "When he saw them he said to them, "Go and show yourselves to the priests." And as they went they were cleansed. [15]Then one of them, when he saw that he was healed, turned back, praising God with a loud voice; [16]and he fell on his face at Jesus' feet, giving him thanks. Now he was a Samaritan.

[17] "Then Jesus answered, "Were not ten cleansed? Where are the nine? [18]Was no one found to return and give praise to God except this foreigner?" [19]And he said to him, "Rise and go your way; your faith has made you well."

Nuff said! I mean, think about it; it's not like Jesus gave them lunch bags full of nourishing food and sent them on their merry way; He cleansed them all of leprosy, which back then was considered a death sentence! Yet, only one of them came back to thank and worship Him, and he was a Samaritan!

So, my question to you is, as His followers and servants, why should we expect anything more?

With that in mind, whenever you encounter ungrateful people, remember they first were ungrateful to our Lord and Savior.

If and when this happens to you, my hope is that you will take comfort in the words the Disciple Peter wrote for all who follow Messiah. If anyone understood suffering for the Cause, it was Peter.

Never forget that we are only visiting this sin-stained planet for a short while. The treasures we'll store up in Heaven for our service to God will be awaiting us on the other side, where they can never be stolen or taken away from us. Know what I mean?

FORGIVENESS

Another thing I've learned along the way is the power of forgiveness. In Matthew 6:14-15, Jesus declared, [14]For if you forgive others their trespasses, your heavenly Father will also forgive you, [15]but if you do not forgive others their trespasses, neither will your Father forgive your trespasses.

I once heard someone say that when you forgive someone who hurts or wrongs you, you free a slave and that slave is you.

Boy, isn't that the truth! Harboring hatred and unforgiveness, on the other hand, is a cancer that will slowly but surely eat away at your soul, not to mention your body and mind. No, thank you.

I can honestly say I have forgiven everyone who has ever wronged me—no matter how great or small the offense. Because of this, I have experienced just how truly freeing it is.

Even more freeing was the day I repented of my sins and received Jesus Christ as Lord and Savior. It was then that the many despicable things I did in life were thrown into God's sea of forgetfulness never to be brought against me again—every-last one of them! It's as if God put up a sign saying, No fishing, Satan!"

I can almost see it in my mind...

Even though I have been eternally forgiven, it doesn't mean I am without sin. Like all Christ followers, the war between my spirit and flesh constantly rages on. Simply put: the old man dies hard.

Because of this, I often find myself asking Jesus to forgive me. Like the Apostle Paul, the things I'm supposed to do at times, I don't do, and the things I'm not supposed to do, I end up doing! Asking for God's forgiveness is almost a daily routine for me.

I also seek the forgiveness of those I've hurt in the past. But with forgiveness being a two-way street, all I can do is ask for their forgiveness, and hope they will grant my sincere request by forgiving me. I also ask God to bring up people I've wronged in the past, people I've forgotten about, so I can get in touch with them.

At the very top of the list is my ex-wife. Even after all this time—and even after being forgiven by God—I'm still ashamed of the terrible things I did to her. She didn't deserve what I put her through. I was completely out of my mind back then!

A few years ago, I wrote a letter begging for her forgiveness and also for the forgiveness of my two sons. I mailed the letter not knowing if I would ever hear back from her.

After six months had passed, I figured she either threw it away or used it as a dart board. Or perhaps she never received it at all...

Lo and behold, a year later I received a phone call. Most people in Florida call me Michael, but when I said hello, she said, "Mike?"

I immediately recognized the voice. It was my ex-wife. I was suddenly nervous; my heart dropped down into my stomach.

She said she received my letter a while back but wasn't sure if she would ever reply to it. I'm so glad she did.

She thanked me for contacting her and said she was glad I wasn't dead and that I was doing well. She then said she forgave me a long time ago and had nothing bad to say about me. She knew my past actions all stemmed from my serious drug addiction.

When she said that, a calming feeling rested upon me. I silently praised God for the way she extended such grace and mercy, when I clearly didn't deserve it.

145

She could have handled it so much differently, but she didn't. She truly is one of the most genuine, caring, and giving people I've ever met. Her actions reminded me of how God extended His mercy and grace to me when I was, and still am, deserving of hell!

Thank you! Thank you! Thank you!

Regarding my two sons, she told them about the letter. But even without it, she assured me that she'd told them long ago that I loved them, but I loved something else even more.

My ex-wife has since remarried. Naturally, in my absence, the boys have come to regard their step-father as the main "father-figure" in their lives. It pierced my heart when I was told they didn't want to reconnect with me in any way.

Do I understand why they said that? Yes, I do.

Do I blame them for saying it? No.

As God's divine providence would have it, I finally got to see my boys, at my mother's funeral of all places. Standing near my late mother's coffin, I looked them both square in the eye and asked for their forgiveness.

Praise God, they both forgave me that day!

Before our brief conversation ended, I told them how truly sorry I was for the many bad choices I'd made, and that I never stopped loving them, despite my serious addiction. I had everything a man could ever want and lost it all because of cocaine.

I told them I wished I could have a 'do over', but that wasn't possible. I said I understood why they didn't want to get to know me, but nothing would ever stop me from loving them.

Three months after my mother's funeral, God opened another door for me, and I flew back home to see my eldest son perform in Wildwood, New Jersey. As it turns out, he is a talented musician. Three of my brothers joined me, along with my nephew, Joseph, and our dear brother, Charles Culmer.

To say I was nervous that day would be an understatement. My twin brother jokingly said, "Let's just hope he didn't write a song just for you!" Not only did we get to watch an awesome performance, my son made sure to spend time with us in between sets. He was just as gracious as my ex-wife was and made me feel perfectly comfortable the whole time I was there. Thank you, Jesus!

I can't help but wonder where God will take our relationship from here. But just knowing He works *all* things for good—not just some—for those who love Him and are called according to His purpose, I'm gripped with anticipation.

What an awesome God I serve!

To my family, I'm truly sorry for what I put you all through. I believe most, if not all of you, have forgiven me. Thank you for that.

For everyone else I've hurt along the way, I wish I could erase the many bad things I did to you all, but I cannot. All I can do is ask your forgiveness and hope you will one day come to see that I'm no longer the vile person I once was.

I pray that by recording many of my past actions in this book, as part of my testimony, God will use it to make a difference in the lives of others. Thank you, JESUS!

TRUE BROTHERS AND SISTERS

Another thing I've learned is what being a true brother or sister really means. Matthew 12:46-50 ESV, says [46]While he was still speaking to the people, behold, his mother and his brothers stood outside, asking to speak to him. [48]But Jesus replied to the man who told him, "Who is my mother, and who are my brothers?" [49]And stretching out his hand toward his disciples, he said, "Here are my mother and my brothers! [50]For whoever does the will of my Father in heaven is my brother and sister and mother."

When I first started this feeding ministry, many from my church, after hearing about what I was doing, were eager to volunteer their time. Members of many life groups have volunteered both time and money over the years. One couple, Tony and Anita Millward, who are part of the life group I attend—and are so dear to me—even donated their van to the ministry.

After a while, the higher-ups at my church, started hearing stories about what we were doing, and helped us move it forward, by supporting us financially.

But it wasn't just members of my church. Many from other churches and Christian organizations have been just as instrumental. A good friend and brother in Christ, Steve Rocca, is actively involved with the Salvation Army. He has been a major blessing to us. Besides donating his time and money—and encouraging many from his church to feed with us—when we were told we could no longer feed at the location we'd fed at for four years, Steve was responsible for finding our present location.

Another awesome story I'd like to share with you happened anonymously. The van that was donated to us was on its last leg, and we were forced to purchase another used van. As it turned out, it needed $1,300 in repairs, and we didn't have the money to fix it.

That same week, someone from California sent a check in the amount of $2,000. I couldn't believe it! Talk about Divine intervention! The timing couldn't have been any more perfect.

With the funds, we were able to have the repairs done to the car and pay for the tags and insurance for the other van we had.

I could literally fill a book with stories of the many who have served with us in some capacity; from donating time and money to Brian and Tammy Saunders dropping off cakes and pastries, to the countless hours David and Rose McNeilly spent working behind-the-scenes, to the many who provided free haircuts for the homeless.

Some have traveled hundreds of miles just to join us. Two church groups drove all the way from Huntsville, Alabama, to Orlando to help us serve. Before the feeding started, the first group helped us reorganize two garages we have for donations.

After that, we fed them the same food the homeless we fed two hours later. They loved it. The second group, who came to Florida many months later, performed for the homeless as they ate their meals. I am grateful to God for all of you. Truly, you are my real brothers and sisters in Christ.

But as I look back, I can honestly say that some of our best volunteers are homeless folks. There's nothing more satisfying than watching the least of these serving the least of these, in Jesus' name.

These people have no money, yet they joyfully give their time and service so freely and willingly.

I'll end this chapter by sharing a story about a man named Joseph. I met him when we worked together at the pizza restaurant. At that time, I was still a babe in my walk with Jesus. Joseph volunteered to feed with me on a few occasions. After the pizza restaurant was forced to close in 2010, due to the sagging economy, we remained friends on Facebook, but we didn't chat much.

In truth, when I saw his many lewd Facebook postings, not about me, but about life in general, I considered blocking or unfriending him a few times.

It seemed we had nothing in common, especially from a spiritual perspective. Then he did an ice bucket challenge and dedicated it to me and *Jesus Loves You Love Him Back*. Pretty awesome, huh?

I messaged him thanking him for still remembering me and my feeding ministry. But the offensive messages on Facebook persisted, and I seriously considered blocking or unfriending him again.

Everything changed for the better after I received a phone call from Joseph in January of 2017. I was quite shocked to see his name appear on my cell phone screen.

After wishing each other a Happy New Year, Joseph asked if he could volunteer with me again.

With a big smile on my face, I said, "Of course! How about this Monday?"

He said that would be great.

Joseph showed up and has since become one of our best volunteers. Even better, he started going to church.

One day he called me saying he was getting baptized at his church and asked if I would like to witness it. What an honor it was for me to see him come up out of the water.

Joseph went on a few road trips with me, but his specialty is shining at those amazing Monday Night feedings.

On a local feeding trip to Kissimmee, he pulled the car to the side of the road and said he needed to tell me something.

Whatever he had to say, I knew it was something serious. He had my full attention.

He told me about his ex-girlfriend, who was a Christian, and the many bad things he did to her. He said they went to Las Vegas in December 2016 for a vacation and got into a bad fight.

When they returned to Orlando, she broke up with him.

Joseph was beyond devastated. His words, not mine.

Unable to cope with the pain, he went out to his garage one night, turned on his car engine. With the garage door closed, he sat there waiting to die. As he sat there, he said the Lord put me on his heart and told him to contact me. That's what he did.

When Joseph told me this, I was totally shocked! I couldn't believe it. I said, "Praise His Holy Name."

I was incredibly humbled and honored to be used by God in that awesome manner. It totally blows my mind that God used me to be a positive influence in Joseph's life.

Thank you, Lord, for trusting me in this matter. May we together keep on jamming for You as long as we have air in our lungs!

Joseph, thank you for allowing me to include this deeply personal part of your life in my book. May it bless all who read it.

CHRISTIAN CONCERTS

Another thing I've learned along the way is that Christian concerts are fun! Not only that, they are just as enjoyable as mainstream concerts, and infinitely more meaningful because of the message the music conveys—especially the lyrics!

As I said earlier, some of my favorite times growing up were the days I went to rock and roll concerts with my twin brother. We would be excited all week waiting for our favorite bands to come to our city. When that day finally arrived, it was party time for us.

Unfortunately, most memories from those days occurred when I was wasted to the point of being out of control of my senses. I would have enjoyed the music so much more had I been sober.

Then again, even if I was sober, that didn't change the fact that I was unknowingly worshiping Satan through the lyrics.

But that was then...

My first Christian concert was a trio band called Phillips, Craig, and Dean. Now that I was following Jesus and I was clean and sober, I was even more excited about going. Even better, it was free to attend!

I picked up my friend on the way to the concert. When I arrived at his house, we high-fived each other and said, "It's time to jam for Jesus."

We listened to Z88.3 the whole ride there. Ever since I could drive, my steering wheel was also my drum set. Nothing changed that night; only the music was different! We jammed to every song they played. Our beverage of choice was either sweet tea or water.

There was no alcohol, no cigarettes, no marijuana, no cocaine, or drugs of any kind. Thank you, Jesus!

The concert was held at Northland Church just outside of Orlando. When we were roughly ten minutes away, we noticed dark, ominous clouds on the horizon. I stopped banging on the steering wheel and paid more attention to the road; the clouds kept darkening and the wind was starting to really pick up.

The moment we pulled into the church parking lot, it started raining cats and dogs. I asked my friend if he wanted to wait it out in the car or make a run for it. Knowing the storm wouldn't be ending any time soon, we agreed to make a run for it.

With lightning striking and thunder cracking all around us, we ran as quickly as we could, jumping over puddles, until we made it to the church lobby.

It was refreshing seeing volunteers handing out fresh towels to everyone, so they could dry off. I certainly don't ever remember ushers at rock concerts doing that.

151

When we found our seats, I looked around and saw moms and daughters, fathers and sons, adolescents, teenagers, and adults of all ages and races. It was beautiful to see.

When the concert started, everyone rose to their feet and the sanctuary erupted in thunderous applause.

Unlike the many rock concerts I'd attended way back when, instead of holding a cigarette lighter skyward along with thousands of others inside the arena, my hands were raised this time for the sole purpose of worshiping Jesus.

I'm sure to some I may have looked like a helpless child wanting to be picked up and held by my Father. They were right!

Jesus did just that!

I believe everyone felt the Holy Spirit in our midst that night. I know I did! I left that concert with a feeling inside I'd never had before. And unlike past concerts, I knew I would remember this one!

Because this was my first Christian concert, it will always be my favorite. But if there was a close runner up, it would be when Laiz and I went to *Night of Joy* at Disney World in 2017, to see some of the top Christian bands perform. It was an outdoor concert.

What made it so special was that it was just two days before Hurricane Irma blew into town. As we worshiped King Jesus, we couldn't ignore the many ominous clouds passing over us, constantly reminding us of what was still headed our way.

Since this was our first hurricane, it was exciting to experience God's power in action. The concert was sold out, but for obvious reasons not too many showed up. Only the die-hards were there.

As sobering as it was, it was equally comforting having the talented musicians up on stage pause on several occasions to pray for the state of Florida. I mean truly pray!

We felt so blessed to be among them that night.

I've been to many Christian concerts since the Phillips, Dean and Craig performance. The one common thread linking them all is that I always leave with a good feeling inside. The musicians are as good or even better than most mainstream groups, but what separates both sides are the lyrics they sing. Both can get my body moving and shaking, but only one side can flood my soul with praise and worship to the King of kings and Lord of lords.

If only I had gone to Christian concerts sooner…

If you haven't been to one yet, I highly recommend it.

MY ROLEX

Another thing I've learned along the way is that the term "valuable jewelry" isn't always what it seems. Case in point: the *Jesus Loves You Love Him Back* wristbands. The many stories I hear about them are nothing short of remarkable.

The reason we ordered them in the first place was to raise funds for the ministry. Not only do we give them away to those who donate to this ministry, we also give them away to the poor and homeless to wear.

The only time I take mine off is when giving it to someone who asks for it. As they slip it on their wrists, I tell them I just gave them my Rolex. Not counting my wedding ring, it's the only jewelry I ever wear. Whenever I give it away to someone, I always feel naked and can't wait to get home, so I can put another one on my wrist.

The stories I hear about the *JLYLHB* wristbands—and have even personally encountered—are more valuable to me than the price of an authentic Rolex watch!

For instance, one of our volunteers named Rebecca had a grandmother living in Indiana. I never met this woman, but she used to follow our ministry on Facebook every day until her death.

She knew she was dying, so she asked Rebecca to send one of our wristbands to her in Indiana, so she could be buried wearing it.

The best part about this story is that she is with Jesus but when she told me this I couldn't help but get a little emotional.

Then there is a man named Iggy who is a brother in Christ. I know him through a program we both attend at church. Iggy is an EMT driver who sees his fair share of crazy things on the job.

One day he was responding to a call of a possible drug overdose. When he arrived, they found a homeless man at the scene. As Iggy and his team put the homeless man in the ambulance, Iggy rolled up the man's sleeves to administer an IV and noticed he was wearing a *Jesus Loves You Love Him Back* wristband.

The man was barely coherent. Even so, he watched Iggy roll up his sleeve and show him the very same wristband. The homeless smiled and Iggy prayed with him. Pretty cool, huh?

I'm at the point in my life where it was time for the "oh so exciting" colonoscopy. Hey, at least my problems are behind me.

On a serious note, my father died of colon cancer, so I decided as a precaution to have it done. I was so nervous my blood pressure shot through the roof and this was just during the scheduling of the colonoscopy. My wife drove me there on the day of the procedure.

As the nurse was prepping me, he noticed my *Jesus Loves You Love Him Back* wristband. He said that three years ago he met the man who started this ministry at a tire store. He said we talked for a half hour about Jesus and the ministry.

I turned to him and said, "That was me."

He looked at me and said, "Yes, it was!" We high-fived each other and he said, "Brother, I'm going to take extra good care of you."

When he said that, it relaxed me big time.

Another man from Orlando donated $20 on our website a while ago. A short while later, he called me asking where his T-shirt was.

After I asked what T-shirt he was talking about, he said the shirt he was supposed to receive for the $20 donation.

I apologized saying we didn't have any shirts for sale at that time and asked if he would like me to refund his donation. He said yes.

The next day I mailed him a check for $20 and included a *Jesus Loves You Love Him Back* wristband for the inconvenience.

Approximately two weeks later, he sent a letter with the check I sent him (he never cashed it), and another check made out to the ministry in the amount of $50. He said when he saw the wristband, he realized we were the same ministry that had fed and clothed his son, who was homeless for many years.

He said he wished he could give more to us. He encouraged me to keep up the good work and that we were truly making a difference. He then said his son was doing better and we were a big reason why!

Finally, there was a woman named Colleen who saw one of the trainers at her health club wearing a *Jesus Loves You Love Him Back* wristband. After inquiring, he told her about the feeding ministry.

One Monday she came down to volunteer her time and has been with us ever since. She's even on the Board of Directors.

I could go on and on. But if God can use something as simple as a rubber wristband to bring so many people together in Christ Jesus, how much more can He use you?

SAVED NOT BY WORKS BUT UNTO THEM

When I first heard St. Francis of Assisi's words to "Preach the Gospel and if necessary use words," it made perfect sense to me. I was new to the faith and really didn't know how to talk to others about Jesus, except through my testimony.

For many years, because of my lack of knowledge of the Word of God, I put Francis of Assisi's words to the test and let my actions be my gospel. I even used Scripture to bolster this claim I wholeheartedly believed.

James 1:27 proclaims, "Religion that God our Father accepts as pure and faultless is this: to look after orphans and widows in their distress and to keep oneself from being polluted by the world."

James 2:14-18 states: "What good is it, my brothers and sisters, if someone claims to have faith but has no deeds? Can such faith save them? [15] Suppose a brother or a sister is without clothes and daily food. [16] If one of you says to them, "Go in peace; keep warm and well fed," but does nothing about their physical needs, what good is it? [17] In the same way, faith by itself, if it is not accompanied by action, is dead. [18] But someone will say, "You have faith; I have deeds." And in verse 26, James wrote: "As the body without the spirit is dead, so faith without deeds is dead."

How could I not believe and fully embrace St. Francis of Assisi's words when it was right there in black and white?

But the more I read the Bible and spent time with those who were more mature in the faith than me—meaning they had a deeper understanding of the Word of God—the more God used these individuals to help me have a better understanding regarding this all-important matter.

One day after sharing with my twin brother that someone told me those who believe St. Francis of Assisi's words to "Preach the Gospel and if necessary use words," were dangerous Christians, my brother said they may not be dangerous Christians, per se, but they do preach a dangerous doctrine, because, in essence, it conveys that the Gospel message isn't enough to save a person, that we also need to perform certain good works, just in case.

My brother then reminded me of Romans 10:14-15, which declares: "How, then, can they call on the one they have not believed in? And how can they believe in the one of whom they have not heard? And how can they hear without someone preaching to them? And how can anyone preach unless they are sent? As it is written: "How beautiful are the feet of those who bring good news!"

Then in verse 17, the Apostle Paul puts an exclamation point on it, when he wrote, "...faith comes from hearing the message, and the message is heard through the word about Christ."

Lastly, my brother reminded me that James—who happened to be the half-brother of Jesus—addressed those in his letter as brothers and sisters. In other words, he was writing to those who were already redeemed by the blood of Jesus and had already crossed over from spiritual death to life.

So, in the final analysis, being saved not by works but unto them simply means the good things we do after we are saved are by no means the root of our salvation, but merely the evidence of it.

With that in mind, if you aren't yet a true follower of Jesus Christ, meaning you've never been born again, it's extremely important that you understand that your good deeds—noble as they may be—cannot bring you closer to God. Only faith in Jesus can.

Romans 6:23 proclaims, "For the wages of sin is death, but the free gift of God is eternal life in Christ Jesus our Lord."

What this means is, regardless of sin—lying, cheating, stealing, bearing false witness, gossip, greed, slander, pride, homosexuality, pornography, drug abuse, alcoholism, gluttony, adultery, murder, lust, premarital sex, it's all sin!

Notice the above Scripture doesn't say the wages of "some of those sins" is death, it says sin, period! All sin!

James 2:10 declares, "For whoever keeps the whole law and yet stumbles at just one point is guilty of breaking all of it."

In other words, if you commit even just one sin, in God's eyes, you're guilty of committing them all. And since we're all sinners, we all stand condemned before a just and holy God.

The only thing that can save us from our sins and from God's wrath is what Jesus did on the cross 2,000 years ago for *all* who would believe in Him! All other roads lead straight to hell.

I often hear from the many homeless people we feed that they can see God working in and through us. And that's a good thing. But if they receive our food and clothing but reject the Gospel message we preach, grateful as they are for the food, it won't bring them closer to Heaven, only closer to hell.

In other words, seeing Jesus in us does nothing to save their soul from utter destruction. You must be born again!

157

The same is true for the many who volunteer with us. You know how much I love you all. So much so that I must caution those of you who may not be born-again, that if you leave this planet without first trusting in Jesus as Lord and Savior, all your good deeds will amount to nothing more than chasing after the wind.

I know many of you are true Christ followers. But if you are not, the fact that you represent this Christian organization cannot and will not make you right with God. Even if you selflessly help us feed another 250,000 homeless people in the coming years, if you haven't been transformed by the Gospel message—meaning you haven't been regenerated by the power of the Holy Spirit— you will stand condemned in your sins before God Almighty someday.

Scary, I know, but it's 100 percent true...

As for myself, I'm mindful of the fact that if I feed the homeless all the days of my life, yet I fail to preach the Gospel of Jesus Christ to them—I'm not talking about sharing my testimony only but testifying for Him—my work for the Kingdom will have been wasted in vain.

Even though I am saved, if they end up in hell because I failed to teach them God's redemptive plan for sinners through Christ Jesus, in a way that everyone could easily understand it, I will surely have to give an account for it.

But this is true for all Christ followers. Whether God calls you to preach or teach or write books or play music or sing songs or feed the homeless, whatever; the service for which He equipped you is secondary to preaching the Gospel to everyone within your reach.

If we do not share Christ crucified with them, how can they hear? How can they know? How can they be saved? Nothing should matter more than this!

Here's what I'm getting at: regardless of how talented you may be in the eyes of the world, if there is no Gospel message being preached over and above the talent God blessed you with at birth—

I'm talking about the Gospel that confronts sin and leads to repentance—there can be no salvation.

From an eternal perspective, your work will have been wasted in vain. I pray no one reading this will travel down that road...

With that in mind, I am committed to preaching the Gospel of Jesus Christ above all other things until my King calls me Home on that great and glorious day. How about you?

IT'S ALL ABOUT THE CROSS

For those of you who still may think the reason I have eternal assurance has something to do with feeding the homeless, with all due respect, either you didn't read the previous paragraphs, or you do not have a clear understanding of the Gospel of Jesus Christ.

Ephesians 2:8-9 declares: "For it is by grace you have been saved, through faith—and this is not from yourselves, it is the gift of God—not by works, so that no one can boast."

John 5:24 states: "I tell you the truth, whoever hears my word and believes him who sent me has eternal life and will not be condemned; he has crossed over from death to life."

Acts 4:12 says: "Salvation is found in no one else, for there is no other name under Heaven given to men by which we must be saved."

John 6:37 proclaims: "All those the Father gives me will come to me, and whoever comes to me I will never drive away." And in verse 44, Jesus declares, "No one can come to me unless the Father who sent me draws them, and I will raise them up at the last day."

There it is in black and white: The salvation God freely offers has nothing to do with humanity and everything to do with Jesus, the very One who lowered Himself from Heaven to rescue everyone on Earth that the Father would send to Him.

In the final analysis, as spiritually dead sinners from birth, only the Most High God can raise anyone from the dead, and point us to His Son. What this means is we do not choose God—He chooses us!

But the Bible also declares that God will never turn away anyone who sincerely seeks Him with all their heart, mind and soul.

Jeremiah 29:13 says all who seek Him *will* find Him—not *many* but *will*! So, the question is, are you seeking God that way?

One thing I've learned since forming my feeding ministry is that while it's true that Jesus does love us—as we boldly proclaim on the shirts we wear and on the lunch bags we hand out—for those who aren't truly born-again, His love has an expiration date.

In other words, for those who are perishing, God's love is conditional. For example, whether you love God or hate Him—faithful servant or staunch atheist—He will provide seed, then send sun and rain to water and grow your crops, not to mention a multitude of other things we humans often take for granted.

But this can *never* be mistaken for unconditional love. If you want to see first-hand the difference between the two, try dying in your sins. If you do that, instead of being welcomed Home as one of God's children, you will feel the full weight of His fierce eternal judgment constantly bearing down on you in a place called hell.

Certainly not unconditional love by any stretch of the imagination. Wouldn't you agree?

But the Good News is, if you truly are saved and you belong to Christ Jesus, you will experience God's unconditional love in such great abundance that it could never be measured in worldly terms.

Not only is God's love unconditional, it's eternal! Imagine being completely smothered by God's unceasing love, while living in perfect peace and harmony for all eternity, when life on this fallen planet comes to an end...

That's precisely what's in store for all whose names are found written in the Lamb's Book of Life! HALLELUJAH!

Now, when it comes to describing God's eternal domain, like all Christians, my knowledge is extremely limited. The Bible provides us with many clues, but certainly not enough to form a complete composite. But if the Earth is God's footstool, how indescribably majestic will Heaven be for all who end up there?

To quote Bart Millard from *Mercy Me*, "I can only imagine..."

But here's something I do know: we will not be turned into angels sitting on clouds playing harps like some naively believe. Not even close! Instead, the gifts God placed in you for His glory and for the furthering of His Kingdom here on Earth are the very things we will bring into eternity with us, including our personalities.

What this means is once you step into eternity, you will still be you; not the sinless version of yourself, but the redeemed version, personality and all!

I don't know about you, but that excites me very much, especially knowing I will be there with all my brothers and sisters in Christ, where we will remain forever and ever. Amen!

Imagine looking and feeling our very best in a place where we will never grow tired of worshipping God the Father, Jesus the Son, and the Holy Spirit. The very thought of it puts a smile on my face.

On a personal note, of all the gifts and skills God has equipped me with, the one thing I won't do in Heaven is feed the homeless! The day I slip into eternity, my services in that capacity will no longer be needed, as no one ever hungers or thirsts in Paradise. Nor will we ever again shed tears or get sick or battle boredom.

And no one will be homeless there! How awesome is that!!!

I hope to see everyone who reads this book there someday...

But until that day comes, there is much work to do for the Kingdom here on Earth. The harvest is plentiful, but the workers are few. As God's co-laborers, we should expect our share of persecution along the way. The world will hate and persecute us just like they did to Jesus. Do not be surprised by this...

But never forget: Jesus never promised an easy life for any of His followers. In fact, He commanded us to deny ourselves and carry our crosses daily and follow Him. But just knowing we win in the end makes all the suffering on this side of eternity—past, present and future—worthwhile.

So, as I finish writing this book, let me encourage you to never cease in using the gifts and talents God chose just for you, to the best of your ability! If you'll only do that, my dear brothers and sisters, you will fully come to understand that the treasures God

161

promises His children aren't earthly temporal things, as some believe, but eternal blessings which will remain with you always.

And the more obedient you are to His calling for you in this life, the greater your reward in Heaven will be.

Even better, the moment you arrive in Paradise, not only will you hear Jesus say, "Well done good and faithful servant"—which should be the goal of all Christ followers—you'll get to see for yourself that God truly is love, as the Bible clearly states.

In fact, it will be impossible to overlook it, because you will become the object of His limitless love! And what can be better than that! Can I get an Amen? Thank you, Jesus!

Matthew 6:19-21 (ESV) declares: "Do not lay up for yourselves treasures on earth, where moth and rust destroy and where thieves break in and steal, but lay up for yourselves treasures in heaven, where neither moth nor rust destroys and where thieves do not break in and steal. For where your treasure is, there your heart will be also."

Epilogue

ALL I KNOW IS...

...I couldn't stop doing cocaine. Now, because of Jesus, I'll never do cocaine again.

...I had a nicotine addiction for 30 years. Now I have no desire to smoke cigarettes.

...I used to drink uncontrollably. Now the only beer I will drink is root beer.

...I never praised God, especially in public. Now I praise Him everywhere—in public and in private!

...I used to worship Satan through the music I listened to. Now I worship only Jesus! As one of God's children, this will continue forever!

...I would talk to everyone I knew about everything but Jesus. Now Jesus is all I talk about!

...I used to spend all my time, energy, effort, and money on bad things. Now I'm a good steward of God's money.

...I was called very bad things back in the day. Now I'm called preacher, pastor (which I am not), and a true man of God.

...I used to get evicted from apartment complexes. Now they ask me to stay even after the lease is up.

...my utilities would get shut off all the time. Now they're always paid on time.

...I couldn't get a bank account back in the day due to my crooked ways. Now I have several accounts. There may be very little money in them, but at least I have them.

...I was never offered credit cards in the past. Now I receive offers all the time. Most I turn down.

...I was told by so many that I couldn't be trusted. Now I am trusted by many.

...I constantly gawked at pornographic magazines. Now I read the Bible daily.

...I would go to strip joints and bars to get my fill. Now I only go to church to get my fill.

...I spent lots of money on plastic baggies filled with white powder. Now I fill them with sandwiches for the least of these.

...I used to drive hundreds of miles stoned out of my head. Now I drive hundreds of miles feeding the homeless and testifying to the least of these in many cities.

...I used to hang out with the turkeys. Now I fly with the eagles!

...I once was blind and now I see!

...I had four cocaine-induced seizures, before Jesus broke that chain. I've had none since...

...there was a time when I could never get a day clean, but that was a very long time ago...

...I deserve 0% of the praise and Jesus gets 100% of all the Praise, Honor, and Glory!

...I can honestly say I have been cocaine and nicotine free for more than a decade now. Jesus broke those chains! Most importantly, God saved my soul from utter destruction by sending His only begotten Son to die in my place.

How could I not praise God with all that is in me? Thank you, FATHER! Thank you, JESUS! Thank you, HOLY SPIRIT!

Though I'm still a work in progress, and I admit I have a long way to go—I'll even go so far to say that I'm still my own worst enemy at times—according to Second Corinthians 5:17, which states, "Therefore, if anyone is in Christ, he is a new creation. The old has passed away; behold, the new has come," I'm a new creation.

Are you? My prayer is that you are...

Thanks for taking the time to read my book. I would be most grateful if you shared your thoughts on Amazon. Even a short review would be appreciated.

To order in paperback, or for bulk discounts, go to www.lovehimbackbook.com. Thank you and God bless you in advance. We post updates about *Jesus Loves You Love Him Back* ministry daily, as well as any promotions we are offering.

Each book sold will bless three homeless people, or anyone else in need of a nutritious meal.

To contact Michael Higgins: higginsmichael11@yahoo.com.

Be sure to read *The Unannounced Christmas Visitor*, winner of the Readers' Favorite 2018 Gold Medal Award in Christian fiction. The story was written by my twin brother, Patrick Higgins, and was inspired by Hebrews 13:2, "Do not forget to show hospitality to strangers, for by so doing some people have shown hospitality to angels without knowing it."

My brother also gathered inspiration for his book while volunteering his time with us, to the extent that he used this ministry as a backdrop for his story. This amazing story will stir your soul like never before, guaranteed! My brother also wrote the award-winning prophetic end-times series, *Chaos in the Blink of an Eye*—which is being favorably compared to the *Left Behind* series.

TESTIMONIALS

The true story of Michael Higgins has been a real inspiration in my life. Meeting Michael and getting involved with the ministry has had lasting effects on my life, being a doer of God's Word. The transformation in this book is evident by the author's life-changing actions! This book is a must-read for anyone looking for "the more to life…"

Kevin Atchoo – Real Estate Broker/ Brother in Christ

I've known Michael now for 5 years and only the power of the Gospel can change a heart like Michael demonstrates now as he lives for the Lord. Everything about *JESUS LOVES YOU LOVE HIM BACK* is about the Gospel and honoring God in the name of Jesus.

A brother in Christ - Jeff Bradshaw

I have been a leader in ministry for about 20 years in Celebrate Recovery, and I first met Michael Higgins in 2009 in our church foyer. I was amazed at his testimony and the passion the Lord had given him for the least of these. I knew others in recovery needed to hear Michael's story to give them hope, so I invited him to CR. Since then, we have become best friends, deacon & yokefellow, and co-laborers of Jesus Christ ministering to inmates through CR Inside at a local prison. The Lord redeemed Michael for His purpose. Michael heeded the call of the Lord to start *Jesus Loves You Love Him Back* and has never looked back! Though my work now keeps me out of town most of the time, I continue to support the ministry.

Jeff Parker
Former Board Member, JLYLHB
Deacon, First Baptist Orlando
Support Group Leader Celebrate Recovery - Celebrate Recovery Inside

Early in our walk following Christ, the Lord put Michael Higgins and his ministry in our lives, and we are forever grateful. We have been with *Jesus Loves You Love Him Back* ministry for over 6 years now and it has been so wonderful to see firsthand how God is working through Michael and his ministry. Tami & I had our eyes opened up to serving the "least of these" in our community. We are forever grateful for Michael and all of the wonderful followers of Christ that we have met through the years serving together. We are also grateful to have seen many folks in need fed with not only food, but God's word. We pray that those who are reading this book feel the Holy Spirit as they read about how God has moved in Michael's life. We pray that you are stirred to reach out to those in need and show love to them. You definitely will be richly rewarded.

Brian & Tami Sanders

We want to thank you Michael Higgins for the example you have set in following Jesus passionately and completely. Since starting to serve at *Jesus Loves You Love Him Back*, we have been impacted by the ministry to serve the least of these, right here in the city of Orlando. Each serving is an opportunity to show love in action to those that desperately need Jesus. Your commitment, enthusiasm and energy to serve others by providing their physical needs through a meal and their spiritual needs through sharing the Gospel, has been an inspiration for us to keep running the race God has set before us. We are honored to serve with you. You are a true testimony of the relentless love of God. He never gives up on us and we will never give up on him.

Mauricio & Jennifer Campos
Love in Action Ministry (Matthew 25:35-45)

God has truly blessed *Jesus Loves You Love Him Back* ministry. God has allowed me to come alongside Michael Higgins to love and serve the homeless throughout Florida and the U.S. It has been good to see God's work touching and saving souls for His Glory as well as humbling. I am thankful to the true and living God for allowing me to serve with the ministry that is good soil.

Gilbert Montez- Brother in Christ

I have known and supported Michael and the *Jesus Loves You Love Him Back* organization for about 3 years. I have never witnessed anyone with more passion and energy for our Lord and Savior than Michael Higgins. He is tireless in his efforts to serve the homeless, no matter where he may be at any time. I consider him a dear brother in Christ and will support hid organization for as long as they need my help.

Stephen Rocca
Technical Collaboration Services, LLC
Consultant, Valencia College
Salvation Army Advisory board

Never before have I encountered a more passionate man than Michael Higgins for the love of Jesus. It is a pure joy to see him pour himself into the *Jesus Loves You Love Him Back* ministry. He is relentless in searching for the lost sheep among us. I would recommend reading his new book and more importantly go spend some time with him. Your outlook, love for people and love for Jesus will change you for the better.

Kenny Majors

Michael Higgins is a man who has never gotten over his salvation and all that Jesus Christ has done for him. The debt of gratitude, the fire in his heart, and the love of Christ, compel him to share the love of Christ to the helpless, hopeless, and hurting. God is using this man powerfully for his kingdom. His life reveals and shows how God can take a man from the guttermost and bring him to the uttermost!

Dr. David Hook - Evangelism Training International

Made in the USA
Las Vegas, NV
30 October 2021